THE BATTLE OF MONTGOMERY, 1644

The English Civil War in the Welsh Borderlands

Jonathan Worton

'This is the Century of the Soldier', Falvio Testir, Poet, 1641

Helion & Company

Helion & Company Limited
26 Willow Road
Solihull
West Midlands
B91 1UE
England
Tel. 0121 705 3393
Fax 0121 711 4075
Email: info@helion.co.uk
Website: www.helion.co.uk
Twitter: @helionbooks
Visit our blog at http://blog.helion.co.uk/

Published by Helion & Company 2016
Designed and typeset by Farr out Publications, Wokingham, Berkshire
Cover designed by Paul Hewitt, Battlefield Design (www.battlefield-design.co.uk)
Printed by Hobbs The Printers Ltd, Totton, Hampshire

Text © Jonathan Worton 2016
Images © as individually credited
Maps © Jonathan Worton 2016

Front cover: The cavalry mêlée at the height of the battle of Montgomery. (Illustration by Maksim
Borisov, © Helion & Company Limited). Rear cover: Montgomery castle; A cornet, a junior cavalry
officer, of the Parliamentary army. (Illustration by Maksim Borisov, © Helion & Company Limited)

ISBN 978-1-911096-23-8

British Library Cataloguing-in-Publication Data.
A catalogue record for this book is available from the British Library.

For details of other military history titles published by Helion & Company
Limited, contact the above address, or visit our website: http://www.helion.co.uk

We always welcome receiving book proposals from prospective authors.

Contents

Acknowledgements 4

Chronology of the Montgomery campaign and earlier related events 5

Introduction 7

1 The course of the war in North Wales and bordering England into 1644 13

2 Sir Thomas Myddelton's raid on Welshpool and wider military
events, August 1644 21

3 The Parliamentarian invasion of Montgomeryshire 31

4 The Royalist counter-attack and the widening campaign 40

5 The commanders 46

6 The armies 57

7 In search of the battlefield 73

8 The battle of Montgomery 84

9 Aftermath and impact 93

Colour Plate Commentaries 100

Bibliography 105

Acknowledgements

I am grateful to the following individuals and organisations for assisting in bringing this book to fruition. Ann and John Welton, curators of the Old Bell Museum at Montgomery, allowed me to photograph and facilitated the reproduction of items in the museum's collection; including the panoramic photograph of Montgomery battlefield by Dr Martin Cadman, who I thank for permitting its publication. The Royal Armouries Museum, Leeds, and Eva Bredsdorff, the curator of The Poywsland Museum, Welshpool, enabled the reproduction of the 'Lymore helmet'. Members of staff at the Clwyd-Powys Archaeological Trust promptly and very helpfully responded to my enquiries, and I am grateful to the Trust for providing photographs from its collection. I am further grateful to the Earl of Powis, to The Trustees of the Lymore Estate, and to Tom Till of the Powis Estate Office, for their assistance and permissions in allowing the inclusion of several images. Rhian Davies and Roy Precious were generous in allowing me to include pictures from their private collections. I have enjoyed sharing ideas about the battle of Montgomery with my good friend Martin Hackett, who has also written about the engagement, although, in the spirit of constructive historical debate, our conclusions differ on the location and repercussions of the battle. Two other local historians, Carrie White, and, in particular, John Davies, kindly shared with me details of their research on the historic routeways of the Montgomery area. Finally, I must acknowledge the editorial team at Helion & Company, with whom it has been a pleasure to work in shaping my manuscript into this attractive publication.

Jonathan Worton
October 2015

Chronology of the Montgomery campaign and earlier related events

1644

16-20 May	Royalist field army led by Prince Rupert marches from Shropshire. Beginning of the Prince's northern campaign, eventually resulting in the battle of Marston Moor.
22-23 June	Parliamentarians capture the border town of Oswestry, Shropshire.
29 June	Royalists lay siege to Oswestry.
2 July	Parliamentarian relief force defeats Royalists outside Oswestry.
2 July	Armies of Prince Rupert and the Marquess of Newcastle defeated at Marston Moor, Yorkshire.
4 July	Parliamentarian advance from Oswestry threatens Shrewsbury in Shropshire, the regional Royalist headquarters.
25 July	Prince Rupert returns to Chester.
5 August	Parliamentarians raid Welshpool in Montgomeryshire.
20 August	Prince Rupert leaves Chester to make Bristol his new headquarters.
20 August	Royalists defeated at Ormskirk, Lancashire.
20-21 August	Royalists come off worst in skirmishing around Northwich and Tarvin, Cheshire.
26 August	Royalists defeated at Malpas, Cheshire.
Early September	Parliamentarians beleaguer Liverpool, Lancashire.
3-4 September	Parliamentarians invade Montgomeryshire.
4 September	Royalist munitions convoy captured by Parliamentarians at Newton, Montgomeryshire.
4 September	Parliamentarians occupy the town of Montgomery.
6 September	Parliamentarians occupy Montgomery Castle.
8 September	Royalists counter-attack at Montgomery, most Parliamentarians withdraw to the castle.
8-18 September	Royalists besiege Montgomery Castle.

17 September	Relieving Parliamentarian and reinforcing Royalist armies arrive in the Montgomery area.
18 September	The battle of Montgomery results in a clear Parliamentarian victory.

Introduction

On 26 September 1644, in churches and chapels across London – within the City, Westminster and, south of the River Thames, Southwark, the districts of the Parliamentarian capital then enclosed by a circuit of defensive earthworks known as the lines of communication – public thanksgiving services were held to praise God for the victory of a Parliamentary army over the forces of King Charles I in a battle fought eight days previously in distant mid-Wales, some 200 miles away.

Three days earlier, on 23 September, after dispatches reporting and confirming the victory had been announced in Parliament, the House of Commons passed a motion agreeing and ordering that:

> On Wednesday next, the twenty-sixth of this instant September, being the day of public humiliation [i.e. a day designated for fasting and prayer] thanks shall be given in all the churches and chapels within the line of communication, to the Giver of All Victories; for the great victory it pleased him to give the Parliament forces over the King's forces, at the raising of the siege of Montgomery Castle.[1]

The battle for the possession of the Parliamentarian-held castle at Montgomery, the county town of Montgomeryshire (today forming part of the county of Powys), fought over fields outside the town on Wednesday 18 September 1644, took place as the First, or 'Great', English Civil War between Charles I and his Parliamentary opponents was entering its third year.

The morale-boosting victory at Montgomery came at a propitious time for the Parliamentarian cause. Less than three weeks earlier, in Cornwall Parliament's main field army in southern England led by the Earl of Essex, lord general and commander-in-chief of Parliamentary forces, had been outmanoeuvred, defeated and forced into partial surrender by King Charles's own field army, with the King having played a leading role in directing Royalist operations. The so-called Lostwithiel campaign ended on 2 September when, isolated and trapped around the harbour at Fowey, Essex's remaining 6,000 infantry surrendered along with the army's artillery and supplies. It was in all respects a humiliating defeat for Parliament. Essex himself, who escaped the debacle by fishing boat on 1 September, writing on the 3rd from the safety of Plymouth to his major-general of foot Phillip Skippon, who had remained

---

1   *Journal of the House of Commons*, Vol. 3, 1643-1644, p. 636.

Montgomery Castle today, the focus of the campaign and battle in 1644.

to conclude the surrender, ruefully admitted 'it is the greatest blow the ever befell our party'.[2]

The unexpected regional victory at Montgomery therefore assumed national significance for Parliamentarians. Writing in an era of religious devotion to a readership believing in divine influence in worldly affairs, a journalist of the Parliamentarian-supporting London press looked to 'the mercy of God, who although he take away our table, yet hath fed us (as it were) with the crumbs of it, in yet opening a wide door of hope by the late success in Wales: which doth in most particulars counterpoise that which the King had in Cornwall'. A more matter-of-fact propagandist Parliamentary editorial published at the end of September echoed the view that the effect of the battle of Montgomery would be to atone for Essex's defeat in Cornwall. In a counterblast against the Royalist mouthpiece *Mercurius Aulicus*, *Mercurius Britanicus* trumpeted: 'But now *Aulicus*, what wouldst thou tell us, of some loss in the West: 'tis true, we had some artillery, some powder, some match, some faithless commanders and common soldiers: But cast up your loss at Montgomery, and tell me then'.[3]

Royalists also understood the military significance and political effect of the battle. King Charles had followed up his victory at Lostwithiel with an unhurried return march through Cornwall into Devon, expecting that Essex's crushing defeat would discourage Parliament's commitment to the war. However, the propaganda value of the Royalist defeat at Montgomery served to bolster Parliamentarian morale and resolve. This was recognised by the Irish Royalist Daniel O'Neil, one of Prince Rupert's aides, writing from Rupert's headquarters at Bristol on 3 October:

> We began to hope the members of London [i.e. the Westminster Parliament] would give a good answer to a message the King sent them upon Essex's defeat. But the fate of this unhappy kingdom will not have her misery end soon. For the blow my Lord Byron received near Montgomery Castle and Massey's taking of Monmouth and other little garrisons [operations by the Parliamentary governor of Gloucester in the south Wales borderland] […] has so hardened the Londoners' hearts, that they will hearken to nothing that will peaceably end their troubles.

Acknowledging the regional implications of the battle, O'Neil added: 'My Lord Byron's unfortunate defeat renders us as little considerable in Cheshire,

---

2   J. Rushworth, *Historical Collections of Private Passages of State* (London, 1721), Vol. 5, p. 703.

3   *The True Informer*, 21-28 Sept. 1644; *Mercurius Britanicus*, 23-30 Sept. 1644.

Lancashire and North Wales'.[4] Arthur Trevor, agent to the Duke of Ormonde, the Royalist lord-lieutenant of Ireland, and by 1644 also a close advisor to Prince Rupert, in reporting 'the business before Montgomery' to Ormonde from Chester five days later also reflected on the damaging outcome: 'We are here ordained to be the mocking stock of the war'.[5]

Montgomery was a regionally important and a nationally significant battle of the First English Civil War. It was also the largest battle fought in Wales during the war. With more than 8,000 soldiers engaged, Montgomery was far more significant in numerical terms than the other larger engagements; including the battles fought in south Wales at Colby Moor (Pembrokeshire), on 1 August 1645, involving perhaps 2,500-3,000 men, and in north Wales at Denbigh Green (Denbighshire), fought three months later to the day on 1 November, when at least 4,500 Royalists and Parliamentarians were present if not fully engaged.

Notwithstanding its significance, however, the battle of Montgomery is only occasionally mentioned in general histories of the Civil Wars. Within this limited coverage the wider campaign and resultant battle have tended to be misrepresented and misunderstood. Both Hibbert and Gentles, for example, muddled events by confusingly involving Prince Rupert in the Montgomery campaign (based in Bristol at the time, the Prince in fact played no part), while the mapping in Gentles's *English Revolution* unfortunately placed Montgomery on the wrong side of the Welsh border, in England, in north Shropshire! Bennett also misinterpreted Parliamentarian operations prior to the battle. Barratt, on the other hand, provided a short accurate account of events at Montgomery in his wider-ranging history of the Royalist army.[6]

The first attempt to reconstruct the battle was made by Phillips, in the narrative volume of his two-part *Memorials of The Civil War in Wales and the Marches* published in 1874, a description that has remained the template for writers exploring the subject since.[7] Dore was first among recent writers to reconsider the battle and wider campaign, taking a view of events from the Parliamentary perspective.[8] Gaunt has looked at the battle and its causes and outcome in some detail, both in the local context of the seventeenth century history of the town of Montgomery and in the wider sphere of the Civil Wars

4   T. Carte, *The Life of James, Duke of Ormonde; Containing an account of the most remarkable affairs of his time, and particularly of Ireland under his government: with an appendix and collection of letters, serving to verify the most material facts in the said history. New Edition carefully compared with the original MSS* (Oxford, 1851), Vol. 6, pp. 202-3.

5   T. Carte (ed.), *A Collection of Original Letters and Papers, Concerning the Affairs of England, from the Year 1641 to 1660. Found among the Duke of Ormonde's Papers* (London, 1739), p. 64.

6   C. Hibbert, *Cavaliers & Roundheads: The English at War, 1642-1649* (London, 1993), pp. 181-2; I. Gentles, *The English Revolution and the Wars in the Three Kingdoms 1638-1652* (Harlow, 2007), pp. 223-4, and Map 1 (preface); M. Bennett, *The Civil Wars in Britain and Ireland: 1638-1651* (Oxford, 1996), p. 234; J. Barratt, *Cavaliers, The Royalist Army at War, 1642-1646* (Stroud, 2000), pp. 118-19.

7   J.R. Phillips, *Memorials of The Civil War in Wales and the Marches, 1642-1649* (London, 1874), Vol. 2, pp. 247-52.

8   R.N. Dore, 'Sir Thomas Myddelton's Attempted Conquest of Powys, 1644-45', *The Montgomeryshire Collections, Transactions of the Powys-Land Club* (1961-2), pp. 91-118.

across Wales.[9] Evans and Abram have also contributed useful narratives in pamphlet form, with Abram having looked in some detail at the likely order of battle of the opposing armies. Most recently Hackett has considered the battle in similar short analytical chapters in two battlefield gazetteers.[10] Despite some factual inaccuracies, the three latter authors have somewhat broadened our understanding of the likely course of the campaign and battle, Hackett in particular having reopened the debate about where the battlefield actually lies. However, the general lack of referencing in support of points of fact and arguments of interpretation, albeit perhaps because of constraints imposed by publishers, makes it unclear how far these writers have made use of contemporary sources to inform their reconstructions of events.

A report by the Clywd-Powys Archaeological Trust has usefully contributed to the historiography of the battle, by interpreting the landscape and the finds of battlefield debris. Coupling the Trust's archaeological fieldwork and topographical analysis to the accepted course of events, the report makes a convincing case to identify the likely area of the battlefield, an analysis largely supported and upheld in this present work.[11]

While the battle of Montgomery remains one of the less well known and understood battles of the First English Civil War, this review of the historiography has shown it has not been entirely overlooked by historians. As a result, the battle and its outcome have attracted different interpretations. Gentles, for example, concluded that 'combined with Marston Moor it annihilated the Royalist military presence in Wales and in all England north of the Bristol Channel'; a sweeping statement unjustified by events, given that the Royalist war effort continued in those parts of the kingdom for the best part of two years after Montgomery. Hackett has argued that 'It is very rare that a single action can determine the outcome of a whole war, yet the events of Montgomery in the summer of 1644 were to prove an absolute disaster for the King'. In the short term the defeat at Montgomery was certainly a debacle for Royalism in the Welsh borderlands, generating immediate and longer-term disadvantageous repercussions. Yet to argue that the battle turned the course of the war is to rely more on the 'what ifs' of counter-factual history, and less on the actual course of events. Gaunt, on the other hand, took a more prosaic view of the battle: while it was certainly clear-cut and decisive, Montgomery was only one 'of a cumulative series of [Parliamentary] victories in 1644 which marked a turn in the tide of the Civil War'.[12]

This book aims to deliver a balanced interpretation of events in reconstructing the likely course and nature of the campaign and battle of

---

9   P. Gaunt, "One of the Goodliest and Strongest Places that I ever looked upon": Montgomery in the Civil War', in D. Dunn (ed.), *War and Society in Medieval and Early Modern Britain* (Liverpool, 2000), pp. 180-204; P. Gaunt, *A Nation Under Siege; The Civil War in Wales 1642-48* (London, 1991), pp. 48-9.

10 D. Evans, *Montgomery 1644: The Story of the Castle and Civil War Battle* (Llanidloes, undated); A. Abram, *The Battle of Montgomery 1644* (Bristol, 1993); M. Hackett, *Lost Battlefields of Britain* (Stroud, 2005), pp. 83-97; M. Hackett, *Lost Battlefields of Wales* (Stroud, 2014), pp. 260-71.

11 M.J. Walters and K. Hunnisett, *The Civil War Battlefield at Montgomery, Powys, Archaeological Assessment*, CPAT Report No. 142 (Welshpool, 1995).

12 Gentles, *English Revolution*, p. 244; Hackett, *Lost Battlefields of Wales*, p. 271; Gaunt, 'Montgomery in the Civil War', p. 188.

Montgomery, and of the significant military incidents beforehand. It is the most detailed account to date, explaining the course of events, describing the commanders and armies involved, and, based on current archaeological, topographical and historical evidence, proposing the most likely location for the battlefield.

While the focus and culmination of this book is to provide a full and fresh account of the battle of Montgomery, it also sets out to place the battle in the context of the First English Civil War as it unfolded in mid and north Wales and bordering England. This theatre of operations was widely fought over, but has been underrepresented in the history of the period. The geographical ambit of this book is therefore mostly the mid and northerly counties of Wales and the adjacent English counties of Shropshire and Cheshire. The borderlands here formed the northerly sector of the Welsh Marches, historically a strip of often-contested territory running the length of the Principality's border with England. In the seventeenth century the six counties of North Wales were the historic shires of Anglesey, Caernarvonshire, Merionethshire, Denbighshire, Flintshire, and Montgomeryshire, with the three latter counties bordering England. Montgomeryshire, the main focus this book, and Merionethshire were geographically more part of mid-Wales.

This book has been researched primarily from contemporary published or manuscript sources. However, like most other smaller battles of the First English Civil War, Montgomery is not well documented The post-battle dispatches written to the Committee of Both Kingdoms, Parliament's war cabinet based in London, from Montgomery on 18 and 19 September 1644 by the joint Parliamentarian commanders Sir John Meldrum, Sir William Brereton and Sir Thomas Myddelton would seem to offer historians an invaluable source of first-hand information. The dispatches were read in Parliament on 23 September and published verbatim in pamphlet form the next day because of their propaganda value.[13] Indispensible as these three letters are – and without them very little indeed would be known about the battle – they provide very little tactical detail or topographical information. Understandably, as devout men in a religious age affected by the euphoria of victory, but perhaps also experiencing post-battle shock, the correspondents instead looked to divine spiritual intervention in explanation. Brereton, for example, saw the turning point of the battle as 'God's opportunity to magnify His power', but does not elaborate as to how the resultant decisive Parliamentarian counter-attack came about.

On the opposing side, the post-battle report written to Prince Rupert by the Royalist commander Lord Byron is lost to posterity and unrecorded. In fact nothing is known of Byron's leadership or direction of the battle. Arthur Trevor's is the only near first-hand Royalist account. Written at Chester on 23 September to inform Trevor's patron the Duke of Ormonde, he based it on conversations with Byron and with his brother Colonel Marcus Trevor, who had commanded a cavalry regiment at the battle.[14]

---

13 *Journals of the House of Lords*, Vol. 6, 1643-1644, pp. 713-16; *Letters From Sir William Brereton, Sir Thomas Middleton, Sir John Meldrum, Of the Great Victory (by God's providence), given them in raising the siege from before Montgomery-castle* (London, 1644).

14 Carte, *Collection of Original Letters and Papers*, p. 64.

Other snippets of second or third-hand information that can be pieced together to reconstruct events are found in the letters of Royalist commanders among Prince Rupert's correspondence, and in the many weekly journals or newsbooks – the newspapers of the time – published mainly in London. This reporting tended to re-work and embellish the tripartite dispatches of the Parliamentarian commanders, but some editorial contains additional information that seems to have been derived from the correspondence of lesser, now unknown, Parliamentarian officers who had been at Montgomery.

Two other contemporary secondary accounts are also useful. The wartime memoirs, in effect a diary, of the Cheshire Parliamentarian Thomas Malbon were edited and published in the 1880s. A Parliamentarian committeeman based at Nantwich, the main Parliamentarian stronghold in Cheshire throughout the First Civil War, Malbon, whose two sons served in Sir William Brereton's Cheshire forces, was a probably well-informed observer of events. The lawyer and political official John Rushworth, who during the First Civil War acted as an 'embedded journalist' with Parliamentarian armies and became personal secretary to Oliver Cromwell, later turned historian to research his eight-volume *Historical Collections* covering the period 1618-1648. Rushworth intended to compile as true a history of the times as possible, and his relation of events at Montgomery is a balanced account that probably drew on several sources.[15]

Finally, a fresh source referred to here that has hitherto been overlooked is what appears to be another Royalist account, transcribed by the mid-Victorian Welsh antiquary Parry from an incomplete contemporary manuscript, now lost or destroyed, among the papers of the Mostyn family of Flintshire. The Royalist Sir Roger Mostyn (1623/4-1690), during the First Civil War was one of King Charles's youngest colonels and the governor of the town and castle of Flint. While it is impossible to link the original to Sir Roger, nonetheless Parry's transcription records a well informed first or near second-hand account of events prior to the battle of Montgomery.[16]

Throughout this book dates have been given according to the Old Style (Julian) Calendar, in use across the British Isles at the time of the Civil Wars. However, the New Year is taken to begin on 1 January, not 25 March as was customary then. Spellings in contemporary manuscript and printed texts have been modernised to aid readability along with some minimal intervention in punctuation.

---

15   T. Malbon, 'Memorials of the Civil War in Cheshire and the Adjacent Counties by Thomas Malbon of Nantwich, Gent', (ed.) J. Hall, *The Record Society for the Publication of Original Documents relating to Lancashire and Cheshire* (1889), p. 147; Rushworth, *Historical Collections*, Vol. 5, pp. 746-7.

16   E. Parry, *Royal Visits and Progresses to Wales and the Border Counties of Cheshire, Salop, Hereford and Monmouth* (London, 1851), p. 386.

1

The course of the war in North Wales and bordering England into 1644

The partisanship that made possible a civil war between King Charles I and Parliament developed uncertainly and haphazardly in North Wales and bordering England as elsewhere in the kingdom during summer 1642. From his headquarters at York, King Charles sought to gain military advantage by nominating commissions of array for each English and Welsh county. A commission named prominent or influential gentry, headed by peers of the realm, who, it was expected, could be relied on to rally support for the King in their locality. In each county the immediate objectives of the commissioners were twofold: to ensure that the militia of the trained bands and the armaments kept in county magazines both came under the control of Royalists.

In Montgomeryshire, control of the magazine had already come into play during the political crisis developing over winter 1641/2. Against the background of widespread fear of a Catholic uprising in England and Wales like that which had engulfed much of Ireland after the native Irish Catholics had risen in October 1641, Sir John Price of Newtown Hall, the MP for Montgomeryshire, organised the removal of the county magazine from the town of Welshpool to Newtown, where Price had local influence. From December 1641 into February 1642 a defensible magazine was constructed at Newtown on the site of the town's long abandoned medieval earthwork castle.[1] Price's action was based on fears that Percy Herbert, son of local magnate William Herbert, first Baron Powis of the Red Castle (known today as Powis Castle) near Welshpool, was preparing to transfer arms from the county magazine to his father's castle. Stories of mass atrocities in Ireland had raised fears of similar carnage on the British mainland to such a near frenzied pitch, that Price and his followers believed that Percy Herbert, a known Catholic who held military authority as a deputy lord lieutenant of Montgomeryshire, was involved in a plot to receive into Wales an army from

---

1   Anon., 'The Price Correspondence of Newtown Hall', in *Collections Historical and Archaeological relating to Montgomeryshire and its Borders* (1900), pp. 104-5.

Colonel Richard Herbert, later second Baron Herbert of Cherbury (*circa* 1600-1655). Herbert led the King's party in Montgomeryshire in 1642 and was a militarily active Royalist, raising a regiment of foot and a troop of horse. (Portrait *circa* 1640 by Cornelius Janssens van Ceulen. © National Trust Images)

Ireland that would support the King against Parliament. Percy may in fact have been acting to secure the arms against civil unrest, but he was summoned by Parliament to London and held there under restraint for about eighteen months before being released on bail.

Montgomeryshire was the first Welsh county to receive a Royal commission of array. Appointed by the King at York on 20 July 1642, this group of 18 likely leading Royalists was headed by another resident magnate, Edward, Lord Herbert of Cherbury who was related to the Herberts of Powis. The Herberts and Prices were traditional enemies, and so that summer Sir John Price withheld the main magazine at Newtown from the Royalist party led by his fellow MP Richard Herbert, son of Lord Edward, who represented Montgomery, the county town. With his followers Richard Herbert did, however, seize and secure at the Red Castle the remainder of the Welshpool magazine, presumably with William Herbert's support. Meanwhile, the Parliamentarian high sheriff of Montgomeryshire refused to publicise or act on the King's proclamations. This impasse, which had probably not involved any loss of life, came to an end when King Charles and his army entered neighbouring Shropshire in the third week of September. By then most of the region in question here was siding with the King. Montgomeryshire passed quietly to Richard Herbert and the commission of array, and Sir John Price shifted with the tide of events and turned Royalist. Richard by then held the King's commission to raise a regiment of infantry.[2]

Until summer 1644 Montgomeryshire would remain a relatively undisturbed backwater of the war, administered by the commission of array. Other than military taxation, the main demand made on the county was to provide recruits. As well as Richard Herbert, three other Royalist colonels came from Montgomeryshire. John and Arthur Blayney of Gregynog, who in turn held the post of the King's high sheriff in Montgomeryshire, in 1643 and 1644 respectively, raised units of horse and dragoons. These seem to have remained just local policing militias, however. Sir Charles Lloyd, scion of another Montgomeryshire landed family and a pre-war professional soldier, took over Sir Thomas Salisbury's Denbighshire regiment in 1643, but he spent the war away from Montgomeryshire and became military governor of Devizes (Wiltshire).[3] Many recruits from Montgomeryshire went to regiments serving much further afield, including to the King's Oxford Army. In March 1644, for instance, orders were sent from Oxford to conscript 134 Montgomeryshire men, and in July for Richard Herbert, Arthur Blayney and others to impress 134 more.[4] Many similar levies and recruitment drives

---

2   *Journals of the House of Commons*, Vol. 2, 1640-1643, pp. 743, 762; *Calendar of State Papers, Domestic Series, of the Reign of Charles I* [hereafter *CSPD*], *1641-1643*, pp. 378-9.
3   N. Tucker, *North Wales and Chester in the Civil War* (Ashbourne, 2003), p. 167.
4   The Bodleian Library (BDL), Dugdale Manuscripts 19 [2nd part], folios 71, 79.

across the Principality since 1642 had made it known as 'the nursery of the King's infantry'.

By the end of 1642, Royalists had gained control in North Wales and bordering England. They had secured strongholds and military resources and begun to establish para-military administrations. Apart from a few armed confrontations, so far there had been no real fighting. Almost the entire Principality had visibly, if not wholeheartedly, sided with the crown. Only in far south-west Wales, in an enclave based on Pembroke, had Parliamentary supporters gained the upper hand. Shropshire was reliably Royalist, although in Cheshire the King's followers only securely controlled the city and immediate hinterland of Chester.[5]

The war in the region began in earnest in Cheshire at the end of January 1643, when the county's leading Parliamentarian Sir William Brereton went on the offensive there. By summer, fighting had spread across Cheshire into north Shropshire and easterly Flintshire between Brereton's forces and the regional Royalists led

Sergeant-major-general Sir Thomas Myddelton, appointed on 12 June 1643 as Parliament's commander-in-chief of North Wales. (Likeness on Myddelton's funerary monument in St. Mary's church, Chirk)

by Arthur, Lord Capel, a Hertfordshire peer. Since March Capel had been the King's regional commander-in-chief, as lieutenant-general of Cheshire, Shropshire, Worcestershire and the six counties of North Wales. In mid-April and again in early August Capel mounted large-scale operations against Nantwich in Cheshire, Brereton's headquarters, but failed to capture the fortified town, while on 30 May Brereton stormed and forced the abandonment of Capel's forward base at Whitchurch in north Shropshire.

In June Parliament put Sir Thomas Myddelton, a wealthy Anglicised Denbighshire landowner, in command of North Wales. But Myddelton's was only a paper command, as the region remained entirely under Royalist control, and he had been forced into exile in London. Nonetheless, Myddelton prepared to take the offensive, and with some small forces but substantial military supplies joined Brereton at Nantwich in August. Together in September they assisted the Shropshire Parliamentarians, another group of exiles, to establish a garrison at Wem in northerly Shropshire, gaining Parliament's first military foothold there. In October Lord Capel with an army about 3,000 strong at first feinted against Nantwich, drawing Parliamentary forces away from Wem, and then rapidly marched south to assault the by then fairly well defended town. The garrison at Wem beat off Royalist assaults on 17 and 18 October and Capel withdrew once Brereton's and Myddelton's relief force drew near. The failure of the Wem campaign had

---

5   The following summary of the course of the war in North Wales and the northern Marches into 1644 reflects the main published accounts. Both volumes of Phillips's *Civil War in Wales and the Marches* remain useful, while the course of events has more recently been revised and reinterpreted by Gaunt in *A Nation Under Siege*; by Tucker's *North Wales and Chester in the Civil War*; and by Hutton in *The Royalist War Effort 1642-1646* (2nd edition, Routledge, 2003), which despite its all-embracing title, is mostly, and very successfully, concerned with the course of the war in Wales and bordering England.

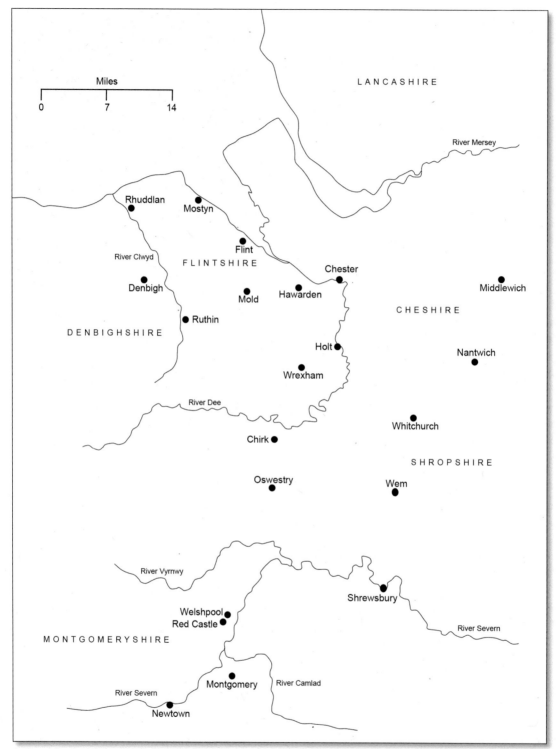

Regional theatre of operations, 1642-44.

not rewarded the effort made to sustain Capel's regional war effort, and many Royalists now lost confidence in his leadership.

Capel's Parliamentary opponents, however, were encouraged to take the offensive. Brereton with Myddelton as his second in command gathered an army more than 2,000 strong, comprising his Cheshire Forces and Myddelton's contingent, together with some Lancashire units, and on 8 November the vanguard entered Wales by storming the fortified bridge spanning the river Dee between Farndon and Holt. The Royalists defending the river line position scattered, and later next day the Parliamentarians occupied Wrexham, an important town in east Denbighshire. From Wrexham the main invasion force pushed on northwards into Flintshire encountering little resistance, reaching the coast and capturing a Royalist fort at Mostyn, while detachments took the castles at Hawarden and Flint. The demoralised Royalists fell back further to the line of the River Clwyd where there were castles at Rhuddlan, Denbigh and Ruthin, although these were probably not readily defensible. It seemed doubtful that the Parliamentarians could be prevented from striking further into North Wales, and Chester was cut off and isolated.

However, the Parliamentarian advance had become over extended, and they quickly retreated in turn when long-anticipated Royalist reinforcements of upwards of 2,500 infantry shipped from Ireland began to land near Mostyn on 19 November. Shunning battle, Brereton's army hurriedly recoiled into Cheshire. At the end of November, a leading Chester-based Royalist was thankfully able to report the end of 'this unhappy interruption of the rebels into Wales'.[6] By then the Royalists had received further reinforcements commanded by John, Lord Byron, sent from Oxford to support Lord Capel. Byron had come as Capel's deputy, but when Capel was recalled to Oxford in December he became the effective regional commander.

Byron wasted no time in taking the offensive. On 12 December he led from Chester an army about 5,000 strong into central and eastern Cheshire. Beating Brereton at Middlewich on the 26th, Byron maintained his winter campaign into the New Year, capturing Brereton's garrisons apart from Nantwich and overrunning most of Cheshire. Notwithstanding the seasonally harsh weather, by mid-January 1644 Byron's army had Nantwich closely besieged. However, a relief army led across the Pennines by Sir Thomas Fairfax, joined by Brereton's forces and a contingent from Lancashire and outnumbering Byron's army, defeated and scattered the Royalists in battle around Acton, just to the west of Nantwich, on 25 January. While Byron fell back to Chester, Fairfax remained in Cheshire for much of February, assisting Brereton to regain the garrisons lost in December and January.

The Shropshire Parliamentarians also took advantage of Byron's defeat by venturing from Wem to establish some outposts. But the regional war shifted once more in the Royalists favour in the third week of February, when Prince Rupert arrived at Shrewsbury to take command as captain-general of Shropshire, Worcestershire, Cheshire, Lancashire and North Wales. With his characteristic energy and organisational and military skill, Rupert reinvigorated the Royalist war effort, making good the ill effects

---

6   Phillips, *Civil War in Wales and the Marches*, Vol. 2, p. 104.

of the defeat at Nantwich. Supported by Byron as an able deputy, as winter turned to spring the Prince's forces, including the original contingent and further reinforcements from Ireland, took the small surviving Parliamentary outposts in Flintshire, put pressure on Brereton in Cheshire, and cleared the enemy from Shropshire apart from their stronghold at Wem.

Prince Rupert also built up a field army based in and around Shropshire, which by mid-April numbered 5,000 infantry and 3,000 cavalry.[7] In May this army had to be put to wider strategic use. In Yorkshire, the Marquess of Newcastle's Royalist Northern Army, under pressure from the north by the Scots army allied to Parliament that had invaded northern England in January, and from the south by the regional Parliamentarian armies of the Northern and Eastern Associations, had fallen back on York, where Newcastle was beleaguered by the end of April. Acting under the King's instructions, during the third week of May Prince Rupert marched from Shropshire, and joining with Lord Byron entered Lancashire. Having once secured the Royalist position in Lancashire and recruited there, the Prince's next and main objective was to cross the Pennines into Yorkshire to assist the Marquess of Newcastle.

Sir Thomas Myddelton had meanwhile spent the early part of 1644 in London, financing, recruiting and equipping a new brigade, larger than the modest forces he had led the previous autumn. In May, Myddelton joined forces in Warwickshire with the Earl of Denbigh, the general in command of Parliament's West Midland Association. Denbigh's association comprised the counties of Warwickshire, Staffordshire, Shropshire and Worcestershire (although the latter was in fact almost entirely under Royalist control). Denbigh was a lacklustre commander, who had been beset by organisational, financial and political difficulties since been given his command at the same time as Myddelton assumed command of North Wales. In May 1644 Denbigh embarked on his first (and what would prove to be his only) campaign, leading from Warwickshire into Staffordshire a small army about 2,500 strong, including units of Myddelton's Brigade. Denbigh's stated objective was to relieve Wem, although the departure of Prince Rupert from Shropshire had lifted the pressure on the garrison. Denbigh had to act under awkward directives issued by the Committee of Both Kingdoms in London. The Committee expected Denbigh to do what he could to support operations against Prince Rupert, while not endangering his regional command. An unexpected advance by the King from Oxford into Worcestershire in early June resulted in Denbigh successfully fighting a defensive engagement at Tipton Green, near Dudley (south Staffordshire), on 11 June.

Paying lip service to the Committee of Both Kingdoms' unrealistic instructions to head north to reinforce the allied armies arrayed against Prince Rupert, Denbigh marched into Shropshire and to Wem. There he agreed with Colonel Thomas Mytton, the commander of the Shropshire forces and Myddelton's brother in law, who, like Myddelton, had fought with Denbigh at Tipton Green, to mount an attack on Oswestry, about 15 miles

---

7   T. Carte (ed.), *A Collection of Letters, Written by the Kings Charles I and II, The Duke of Ormonde, the Secretaries of State, the Marques of Clanricarde, and other Great Men, during the Troubles of Great Britain and Ireland* (London, 1735), p. 278.

The late medieval bridge crossing the river Dee between Holt and Farndon, captured by Parliamentary forces on 8 November 1643. At that time the second span from the right supported a defensive tower and drawbridge.

west of Wem close to the Welsh border. Lord Capel had garrisoned the town in 1643, but although the Royalists had repaired the small castle and medieval town walls, they had not strengthened Oswestry with up to date earthwork fortifications.

Denbigh and Mytton leading about 900 men approached Oswestry around midday on 22 June. After deploying parties of cavalry to cover the approaches to the town, to prevent the garrison's retreat and to give warning of the approach of any relieving force, the Parliamentarians first attacked the parish church. This was situated in a suburb outside Oswestry, but it commanded the town walls and so had been occupied by the Royalists as a strong point. 200 Parliamentary foot stormed the place, and after a fierce, half-hour long skirmish the remaining defenders who had withdrawn into the church tower surrendered. Two cannon were then brought forward and at close range battered down one of the town gates. Another shot struck and disembowelled a townswoman and wounded a couple of the defenders, disheartening the garrison who took refuge in the castle in the centre of town. Their cavalry entered first, and by mid-afternoon the Parliamentarians had secured Oswestry. Effective musketry by its defenders deterred them, however, from launching an immediate assault on the castle, and a short bombardment by the cannon had negligible effect on its walls.

At a council of war Denbigh and his senior officers agreed to storm the castle after burning the gates using pitch. However, when an assault party of dismounted troopers set out to do so next morning, they were obstructed by a crowd of townswomen pleading for the lives of their men folk in the town militia who made up most of the castle's defenders. Denbigh and his officers needed an interpreter to understand the women's agitated 'Welsh howlings', as a Parliamentary commentator uncharitably put it, but the outcome was that the women were allowed to persuade the garrison to enter negotiations and Denbigh accepted the surrender of the castle shortly after. The Parliamentarians reported the capture of about 240 prisoners of war of all ranks, and a haul of weaponry including 100 muskets. The Royalists were found to have just one barrel of gunpowder in the castle, and so could not have prolonged their defence in any case.[8]

---

8   *Two Great Victories: On[e] Obtained by the Earle of Denbigh at Oswestry […] The Other by Colonel Mitton* (London, 1644).

Leaving at Oswestry a strong garrison including 400 musketeers and a troop of horse, Denbigh with his own cavalry went northward into Cheshire to join other Parliamentary forces attempting to shadow Prince Rupert's movements from afar. On 29 June a Royalist force from Shrewsbury about 2,000 strong bringing heavy cannon laid siege to Oswestry, but they were beaten and forced to withdraw on 2 July by a relief force 1,500-1,700 strong led by Sir Thomas Myddelton. On the same day near York the armies of Prince Rupert and the Marquess of Newcastle were beaten at Marston Moor. The Earl of Denbigh had followed Myddelton bringing reinforcements, and on 4 July their combined army numbering 3,500-4,000 men approached Shrewsbury from the west. After a series of skirmishes the Parliamentarians withdrew late that evening, having briefly managed to attack Shrewsbury's westerly outer defences.

The fortnight-long campaign for the possession of Oswestry ended when Denbigh withdrew from Shropshire over the next couple of days. The remaining Parliamentary forces dispersed to their garrisons, and Myddelton based himself at Oswestry. The town gave him at last a potentially secure base on the Welsh border. It was, as Myddelton put it, 'a very strong town, and if once fortified, of great concernment, and the key that lets us into Wales'.[9] It would not be long before Myddelton turned the key and took the war there.

---

9   *A Copy of A Letter sent From Sir Tho. Middleton, to the Honourable, William Lenthall Esq; Speaker of the House of the House of Commons. Concerning the Siege at Oswestree* (London, 1644).

2

Sir Thomas Myddelton's raid on Welshpool and wider military events, August 1644

In mid-July 1644 the Committee of Both Kingdoms authorised Sir Thomas Myddelton to begin military operations in Wales, with the proviso that he was expected to continue to cooperate with his fellow regional commanders. The Committee considered that the military situation in Shropshire was then sufficiently favourable to allow Sir Thomas an opportunity for independent action. This gave him authorisation to put into effect the plans he was already making to take the war across the border. On the 16th, Colonel Thomas Mytton had written in coded terms from Oswestry to inform his wife in London that he planned to transfer troops from Wem to Oswestry, because 'Brother Myddelton and myself intend, God willing, to take a voyage into Wales.'[1]

This would be the first time that Parliamentarians had mounted significant military operations in mid-Wales. The objective of the plans of the brothers-in-law Myddelton and Mytton was the town of Welshpool, lying just a couple of miles over the Shropshire border in Montgomeryshire and also known concurrently to English speakers simply as 'Pool'. The operation they would mount was a characteristic action of the First Civil War, known as a 'beating up of quarters': a hit and run raid against the enemy in his billets or encampment.

Welshpool in itself had no particular strategic value. During the seventeenth century it seems to have been a reasonably prosperous place, and of greater economic importance than Montgomery, the county town. In 1673 Welshpool was described in a gazetteer as being 'in a rich vale, the greatest and best built corporate [i.e. self-governing] town in the county […] it is well inhabited […] its market on Mondays is very considerable for cattle, provisions and flannels'. This summarised the reasons for the town's prosperity. As well as being a marketplace for local agricultural produce, Welshpool was a centre for the production and distribution of woollen textiles (the 'flannels'), which, along with the rearing and trade of cattle,

---

1   National Library of Wales (NLW), Sweeney Hall Manuscripts A1, folio 20.

These three premises fronting onto Welshpool's high street are among the few buildings in the modern town to remain substantially unaltered since the time of the Civil War. Dating from around 1600, they display the decorative boxed timber framing typical of the period.

was the mainstay of the economy of mid and north Wales. An estate map dating from 1629 depicted around 150 buildings in Welshpool, making it a sizeable town for Wales at that time.

To all military intents and purposes, however, Welshpool was indefensible. Apart from a long abandoned and overgrown twelfth century earthwork castle, there were no surviving medieval defences, and because the town had developed along its long and broad main street its linear form was difficult for an occupying force to defend. Bounded by higher ground to the west, north and south, Welshpool lay within a shallow valley that broadened onto the flood plain of the river Severn a mile or so to the east. A stream or rivulet bounding Welshpool to the north, crossed by three small bridges, was a limited obstacle against attack, but the only really defensible stone-built building was the parish church, standing somewhat isolated from the main street at the east end of town north of the rivulet.

Welshpool become a Parliamentarian target in early August 1644 because of the eight troops of Royalist cavalry then quartered in and around the town. Sir Thomas Myddelton saw them as an obstructive occupying force: 'Being sent there expressly by the Prince to prevent the well-affected in that county from joining with me in the present service, and for raising of men for himself'.[2] Probably numbering more than 400, all ranks, most, of the Royalist horsemen were of Prince Rupert's own regiment, recently posted to the Welshpool area to rest and recuperate after returning from the northern campaign.

Under their acting commanding officer, the regiment's major, Sir Thomas Dallison, four troops of Rupert's Horse were billeted in Welshpool itself, while the remaining four troops were quartered in outlying townships (farms and other small settlements). By Dallison's own admission (a dispatch he penned on 4 August as a situation report to Prince Rupert was found by the Parliamentarians in his quarters and later published in a London journal), the regiment's most immediate problem was a shortage of horses: 'We have lost many, by reason of the great march which we have had'.[3] Those remaining were being put to grass during the day and stabled or corralled overnight. Although the Royalists had made portable barricades to obstruct the immediate approach roads to Welshpool, Dallison was aware of his command's vulnerability to surprise attack; his dispatch was intended to

2   *CSPD, 1644*, p. 405: Myddelton's dispatch dated 6 Aug. 1644 reporting the action at Welshpool to the Committee of Both Kingdoms.
3   Published in *The True Informer*, 10-17 Aug. 1644.

advise Rupert of 'our weak estate where we are'. On the other hand, the local Royalist war effort was being mobilised in Dallison's support. The commissioners of array for Montgomeryshire were coming to Welshpool on 5 August to meet with him to make arrangements for the pay and quartering of Dallison's men, and cloth had been made available for new cloaks for the troopers.

This Welsh cloth, together with a consignment of coats and caps, made up in uniform colours, for two regiments of foot in Prince Rupert's regional army, was being stored at the nearby Red Castle. Set on a rocky ridge amid parkland less than a mile south of Welshpool, as has been seen the originally thirteenth-century Red Castle (so-named after its sandstone masonry) was the seat of Sir William Herbert, Lord Powis. Powis was an enthusiastic Royalist and was providing assistance for Dallison. The Red Castle, then, by summer 1644 was a Royalist stronghold, although it had probably only a small garrison. They were likely to have been local militiamen, including Lord Powis's followers and tenants, rather than regular Royalist soldiers.

Acting on accurate intelligence reports, Sir Thomas Myddelton and Colonel Mytton prepared their taskforce to march from Oswestry on the afternoon of Sunday 4 August. Comprising horse, foot and dragoons drawn from Myddelton's Brigade and Mytton's regiments of the Shropshire forces, south of Oswestry they were reinforced by two companies of Cheshire Foot sent from Nantwich. Altogether the Parliamentarians numbered about 600 men, in approximately equal numbers of mounted and foot. Having rested until sunset after crossing or fording the river Vyrnwy, probably in the area of Llansantffraid-ym-Mechan or Llandysilio, the taskforce marched overnight towards Welshpool. Rather than taking the easier route down the Severn valley, instead the Parliamentarians approached from the hill country to the north of Welshpool. This avoided nearing the town from the east, across the Severn's flood plain, where in the darkness the glow from the lit matches of the matchlock musketeers might be seen from a distance; as one of them reported, the Parliamentarians 'marched round about the mountains to gain the town, lest that the lit matches should discover us [...] compassing and gaining the town about break of day'.[4] Another report acknowledged the 'tedious march from Oswestry to Pool which the nearest way is 12 miles (the way that they marched considered) may be accounted less than 24 miles hereabouts'. By modern roads and measurement, on their march the Parliamentarians may actually have covered about 17 miles.[5]

In the early morning of Monday 5 August the Parliamentarians were within a quarter of a mile or so of Welshpool when in the half-light they encountered the enemy. Mounted Royalist picquets exchanged fire with the leading troopers but were unable to delay them, and instead were pursued into the town; Myddelton described 'meeting their scouts, who fired upon us, the van of our horse followed them so closely that they had not time to put up

---

4   This reconstruction of the operation is based on what seems to have been this first-hand account, published in *Wareham taken by the Parliament Forces. Also Collonel Mittons valiant Exploits certified by two several Letters dated at his Quarters* (London, 1644), and also on Myddelton's dispatch to the Committee of Both Kingdoms.

5   *A Perfect Diurnall of some passages in Parliament*, 12-19 Aug. 1644.

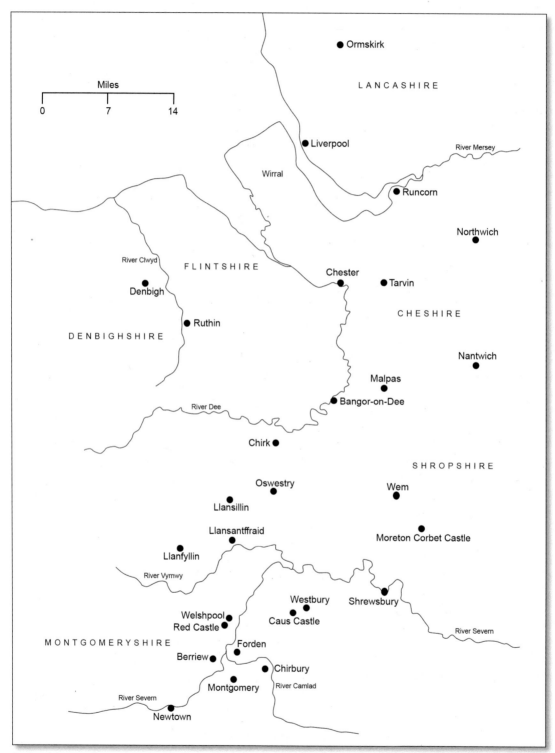

Regional theatre of operations, August–September 1644.

their barricades, and so we entered the town with them'. The Parliamentarians had planned to encircle Welshpool and launch attacks from two directions – a difficult enough operation to coordinate before full daylight – but the engagement of their horse before the foot were in position allowed most of the Royalists to make good their escape, many of them fleeing to the safety of the Red Castle. As Myddelton admitted: 'By reason of the darkness and of our ignorance of the passages between the town and Lord Powis's castle, wherein was a garrison of the enemy, Sir Thomas Dallison with many of his officers and troopers escaped hither'. Although lacking coordination, and by the exchange of gunfire having lost the element of surprise, nonetheless the Parliamentarian raid proceeded successfully. Overrun and scattered, the Royalists offered little resistance, with the notable exception of the cornet of Prince Rupert's own troop who refused to surrender, reportedly 'saying he did scorn to take quarter of such Roundhead dogs as we, and so he was killed in the town'.

Apart from the belligerent cornet, Myddelton reported the loss of 'some few of the enemy's side', five officers and 60 or so troopers taken prisoner, along with two colours and a quantity of weaponry. One of the commissioners of array already in town for the meeting that day was also captured. Although Myddelton may have exaggerated the actual number of horses taken as 200, at this time the Royalists would have found it difficult to replace any significant loss of horseflesh. The other correspondent among the Parliamentarians gleefully related now the Royalists fled: 'some stark naked, some in their shirts, some with their breeches off; in this manner they all save about seventy escaped away leaving their arms and most of their horses behind them; and some of the Cavaliers were taken on horseback […] and some saddling their horses in the stables'. Apparently just one Parliamentarian soldier was killed in the action.

Once the town was secured and the prisoners rounded up, Myddelton and Mytton acted to prevent some small-scale looting by Parliamentary soldiers from becoming widespread. Meanwhile, a mounted detachment was sent to rustle the cattle the Royalists kept in the meadows near the Red Castle. Mindful that the enemy might rally, and with reinforcements launch an attack from the castle, probably shortly after 8.00 am Myddelton and Mytton withdrew their men from Welshpool. With their spoils and prisoners of war they marched unmolested back to Oswestry.

Theirs, as a London newsbook reported, had indeed been 'a piece of good service', and for the Royalists was an unsettling blow in what hitherto had been secure territory and a quiet backwater of the war.[6] Myddelton, like his fellow regional commanders, however, remained apprehensive about Prince Rupert's return to the region: 'We believe he intends to make this the seat of war, devastating the country', he reported to the Committee of Both Kingdoms. The Committee, meanwhile, had recognised that there was a strategic opportunity to strike against the Prince before he could reorganise his army. In early August it attempted to coordinate an ambitious plan, whereby units from the East Midlands and from the Earl of Manchester's Army of the Eastern Association would be redeployed to the Welsh

---

6   *A Diary, or an Exact Journal*, 8-15 Aug. 1644.

borderland. Joining with the Cheshire, Lancashire and Shropshire forces, they would disrupt Rupert's operations and hopefully bring him to battle and inflict a second Marston Moor-like defeat. However, as a result of a council of war with his officers held at Lincoln on 10 August, Manchester in so many words rejected the plan out of hand, citing, not unreasonably, the weakened state of his own regiments, which could only worsen on the march, logistical problems, and the impracticality of besieging Chester, Rupert's current base, without a properly equipped train of siege artillery.[7]

It was thus left mostly to the Cheshire, Lancashire and Shropshire forces to attempt to keep Prince Rupert in check, but the Parliamentarians had in fact overestimated his present capability. On 3 August Sir William Brereton reported to the Committee of Both Kingdoms the subdued and defensive stance of the enemy in the region: 'We conceive they are in much want of ammunition and arms, because they are so little active'.[8] Since returning to Chester on 25 July, despite attempting his usual thoroughgoing approach Rupert had found it difficulty to reorganise and re-recruit the units of his regional army amid shortages of money and military supplies. An intelligence report from Nantwich dated 12 August summed up the weakened and somewhat demoralised state of Royalist forces in the northern Marches:

> Prince Rupert is in Chester, his horse are quartered in the several counties of Chester, Flint and Denbigh and Montgomery […] none of their courage hitherto durst bring any of his forces of horse over the hills beyond Ruthin [Denbighshire] or Flint, and therefore the parties you know of need not fear of his horse. As for the foot, by reason of his wants thereof and daily recruital out of those further parts of Wales beyond the mountains, that are compulsorily brought in daily for recruits, run away as fast back upon the first opportunities.

The desertion of new recruits had become a particular problem. Another newsbook reported that 'Prince Rupert is in Chester, he is diligent to make recruits, some he gets, and some he looseth, for many are gone from him lately', but reckoned that the Prince still intended to make Chester 'the seat of the war in those parts'.[9] Rupert, however, had become dismayed by his situation, and was perhaps also mentally and physically exhausted, having spent most of the last three months on campaign. On 20 August he abruptly left Chester, thus effectively abandoning his regional command to the charge of his deputy Lord Byron. Riding the length of the Welsh Marches escorted by some horse, Rupert arrived at Bristol on the 26th and made the city his new headquarters.[10] At Chester at the end of August, Arthur Trevor confided to the Marquis of Ormonde how since being defeated at Marston Moor, the Prince had been beset with problems: being 'without arms a general of an army'; 'of ordnance without cure, not a gun too, less money, much mutiny'. Stressing the latter problem, Trevor noted that several Royalist officers from

---

7   *CSPD, 1644,* pp. 406, 413, 428, 431.

8   Ibid., p. 394.

9   *The Perfect Occurrences of Parliament And Chief Collections of Letters,* 16-23 Aug. 1644; *A Diary, or an Exact Journal,* 8-15 Aug. 1644.

10 C.H. Firth (ed.), 'The Journal of Prince Rupert's Marches, 5 September 1642 to 4 July 1646', *The English Historical Review* (1898), p. 737; *The London Post,* 3 Sept. 1644.

the Chester garrison had recently defected to Sir William Brereton at Nantwich.[11]

Prince Rupert's departure was soon followed by a series of Royalist reverses in Cheshire and Lancashire.[12] On 20 August, while Rupert was heading to the Royalist garrison at Ruthin on the first day of his southerly journey, Colonel John Marrow, an experienced and charismatic but impetuous cavalry officer, had led a substantial detachment of horse and foot from the Chester garrison in a raid towards Parliamentarian-held Northwich, 19 miles east of the city. Short of Northwich, at Hartford Marrow's force was intercepted by detachments from the Northwich garrison and the nearby Parliamentarian outpost at Crowton. In the resultant confused skirmishing the Royalists took fourteen Parliamentarians prisoner, but in withdrawing eastwards Marrow was wounded in further skirmishing at the village of Sandiway. Evacuated to Chester, Marrow died next day, leaving the men of his own regiment demoralised: as a Parliamentarian report gleefully put it: 'both he and his regiment of horse died at one time'. In the meantime Marrow's force had withdrawn to Tarvin, six miles east of Chester. There, on the 21st, they were attacked by Sir William Brereton with his own regiment of horse and some foot from Northwich. Although a number were captured in the skirmishing around the village, the Royalists resisted by occupying and defending Tarvin's parish church until the arrival of reinforcements from Chester caused Brereton to withdraw.

The escape route taken by Royalist soldiers fleeing from Welshpool on the morning of 5 August 1644 seeking the protection of the Red Castle (now Powis Castle), on the skyline here. This was then an area of parkland and meadow, as it remains today.

Meanwhile, on 20 August some 25 or so miles to the north in southern Lancashire the Royalists had suffered a serious reverse at Ormskirk. Here the Royalist Northern Horse had been forced into fighting a rearguard action against pursuing Cheshire and Lancashire Parliamentarians commanded by Sir John Meldrum. Led by Sir Marmaduke Langdale, the Northern Horse was an amalgamated division of the many small regiments of horse of the Marquess of Newcastle's Northern Army. Rallying under Langdale's leadership after Marston Moor, in later July the Northern Horse had retreated westwards into Cumberland and Westmoreland, but in August began to withdraw southward. Entering Lancashire, they were joined by the Lancashire horse regiments of Sir Thomas Tyldesley and Richard, Lord

---

11 Carte, *A Collection of Letters, Written by the Kings Charles I and II*, p. 349.
12 Contemporary sources for the following actions, near Northwich, at Tarvin, and at Ormskirk and Malpas, include: Malbon's 'Memorials of the Civil War', pp. 141-4; Rushworth's *Historical Collections*, Vol. 5, pp. 745-6; *A True Relation of Two Great Victories obtained of the Enemy: The one by Sir William Brereton in Cheshire, The other by Sir John Meldrum in Lancashire* (London, 1644); and *The Success of Our Cheshire Forces, as they came Related by Sir William Brereton's own pen* (London, 1644).

Sir William Brereton, commander-in-chief of Parliamentary forces in Cheshire throughout the First Civil War. Brereton played a leading role in the regional campaigns during 1644.

Molyneux, which formed a small brigade under Lord Byron's command. This combined force probably numbered more than 2,500 horse, with a few hundred foot of Tyldesley's own regiment.

For the previous few days Meldrum had been tracking and attempting to bring Langdale's division to battle, and on the evening of the 20th caught up with the Royalist rearguard on moorland outside Ormskirk, while their main body was passing through the village. Intelligence reports had led Meldrum to believe that the Royalist cavalry were 'but very badly armed and horsed, and for the greater part without ammunition', and their performance at Ormskirk seems to have reflected this. Making a stand, the Royalists attempted to draw up in battle order on both sides of the village, but a volley or two of musket fire by the advancing Cheshire Foot immediately followed by a charge by supporting horse caused Molyneux's brigade, acting as the rearguard, quickly to break and scatter. The Northern Horse on the far side of Ormskirk did not stand to fight, but a more general rout seems to have been prevented by a detachment led by Langdale covering the retreat of the main body. Lord Byron, who had come from Liverpool with his own regiment of horse to confer with Langdale, and who professed to have 'thought nothing less than fighting that day, as having no intelligence of the enemy being so near', joined Molyneux's brigade and was caught up in their retreat. As he reported to Prince Rupert:

> Sir Marmaduke sent most of his own horse before, and the retreat being made by my Lord Molyneux his brigade, they (according to their accustomed manner), upon a volley of musket shot from the enemy, fell foul in such a fury upon my regiment, that they utterly routed it; and the enemy's horse, taking advantage of the disorder charged […] took and killed some, and struck such a terror into the rest that they could not be stopped till they came to Liverpool.[13]

There were probably few Royalist casualties, but in the rout the Parliamentarians reckoned to have taken about 280 prisoners. Byron and Molyneux reportedly evaded capture by dismounting and hiding for a while amid a field of standing corn. Writing to Prince Rupert from Chester on 22 August, Sergeant-Major William Legge, Rupert's appointee as the city's military governor, viewed the action somewhat differently to Byron. He blamed Byron for in fact having precipitately engaged the enemy with Molyneux's rearguard, and that only Langdale's secondary rearguard action had prevented a worse defeat.[14]

Meeting up with Byron late that evening, Langdale and other senior officers of the Northern Horse rejected his appeals to remain in the northwest. They were instead determined to continue their withdrawal southward, making Oxford their eventual objective – not least because of the perceived difficulty of re-equipping and providing victuals and forage for such a large

---

13 BDL, Firth Manuscripts C7, folio 148.
14 E. Warburton, *Memoirs of Prince Rupert and the Cavaliers* (London, 1849), Vol. 3, p. 21.

body of horse from the limited resources in north-east Wales. With most of the Northern Horse scattered at Ormskirk having rallied to Langdale over the following day or so, and still numbering upwards of 2,000 men, they resumed their southward march into Cheshire. They spent the night of 25/26 August quartered in and around Malpas, probably intending next morning to march to Bangor-on-Dee, about seven miles to the west, to cross the bridge there over the river Dee and so enter Wales and safer territory.

However, at dawn on the morning of Monday the 26th the Royalist picquets a mile or so beyond Malpas encountered the leading units of a substantial force of Cheshire Parliamentarians led overnight from Nantwich by Sir William Brereton, comprising eight troops of horse and seven companies of foot, in all 900 men or more. In the cavalry engagement of charge and counter-charge that developed around the small market town the Northern Horse put up a more determined fight than at Ormskirk, despite suffering a reverse at the beginning of the action when an advanced unit, or 'forlorn hope', was outflanked and broken by the enemy. Parliamentarian reports acknowledged how 'in a brisk encounter', the 'King's forces marched out towards them in good order, and gave them two or three gallant charges', and how they 'found the enemy to stand in six or seven several bodies, or divisions, in very good order'. However, as at Ormskirk, the steadiness and supporting firepower of the Cheshire Foot eventually decided the action, and the Royalists, with Langdale having been seriously wounded, were driven from Malpas in disorder. The still outnumbered Parliamentarian horse did not pursue them far.

In an understandably gloomy dispatch to Prince Rupert written at Chester on 29 August, Lord Byron explained how 'Since Sir Marmaduke Langdale came out of Lancashire another misfortune hath befallen his troops which were beaten up at Malpas […]. The officers did as well as they could but were deserted by their soldiers. Sir Marmaduke is shot in the thigh; he now lies under the surgeon's hand at Chester'. Acknowledging the loss at Malpas of five other officers, Byron wrote of the Northern Horse that 'the rest are marched through Wales, being in such fright that they are not yet fit to come near the enemy'. Pointing to what was becoming a pressing shortage of military supplies, he added: 'I beseech your highness, think of some speedy course to supply us with ammunition, without which we can neither offend the enemy nor long defend ourselves'.[15]

With mobile Royalist forces cleared from Lancashire, and in Cheshire withdrawn to Chester, on 31 August Brereton's forces had begun to establish garrisons to the east of Chester within ten miles of the city. Earthworks began to be built to fortify Tarvin, and manor houses at Huxley and Oulton were occupied and made defensible. Still Royalist-held Liverpool was by then beleaguered, if not yet tightly besieged, by Sir John Meldrum with the Lancashire forces, while being blockaded by Parliamentary warships patrolling the Irish Sea. Meldrum had also received reinforcements of a division of Yorkshire Horse commanded by Sir William Fairfax. Writing to his wife from the Parliamentarian leaguer, or encampment, before Liverpool on 7 September, Fairfax accurately summarised the regional military situation:

---

15   William Salt Library, Prince Rupert's Papers, SMS 486.

'As for the enemy we have beaten them out of the field into their holds. The Prince's army is reduced to a very small number, and what strength they have are all beaten into Wales'.[16]

The string of defeats and setbacks during August, in mid-Wales, Cheshire and Lancashire, compounded by the departure of Prince Rupert and the apparent flight of the Northern Horse, had done great damage to Royalist morale. Although buoyed by his success at Ormskirk, on 21 August Sir John Meldrum, unaware that the Prince had already left Chester, nonetheless still expected him to 'enter the stage and interrupt the game'.[17] Once it generally became known to them that Rupert had in fact abandoned the region, the Parliamentarians would have been encouraged to quickly take action in his absence. These circumstances gave Sir Thomas Myddelton the opportunity to launch the invasion of Wales that was his objective since the capture of Oswestry. Accordingly, one of his officers wrote from Oswestry on 3 September, that 'God willing, tomorrow we are advancing with all our forces into Montgomeryshire. I hope you will hear good news from us'.

---

16   C.R. Markham, *Life of Robert Fairfax of Steeton, 1666-1725* (London, 1885), p. 22.
17   *CSPD, 1644*, p. 443.

3

The Parliamentarian invasion of Montgomeryshire

Sir Thomas Myddelton's logistical preparations were completed when, on or shortly before 30 August 1644, a munitions convoy arrived safely at Oswestry from Wem. *En route* a body of Royalist horse had attacked the convoy, but the escort reinforced by a mounted detachment sent to their aid from Oswestry fought them off. A report of the skirmish described how once Myddelton had received intelligence of the Royalists' approach, he:

> Sent out a party from Oswestry to guard the ammunition, which party discovering the enemy, wheeled into their rear, all the horse [of the escort] being in the van, and fell upon them, killed five upon the place, took five prisoners and wounded many, and made the enemy fly; but being to guard the ammunition, durst not leave their charge to follow them.[1]

As a result of the replenishment of the magazine at Oswestry, on 1 and 2 September eight companies of Myddelton's Brigade, foot and dragoons, were issued with new equipment including almost 200 bandoliers, 250 swords and belts, and 95 muskets, of which half were superior flintlock weapons.[2]

Myddelton would invade Montgomeryshire with only his own brigade, which he later said had numbered about 650 men. However, at the time Lieutenant-colonel James Till, the deputy commander of Myddelton's Regiment of Horse and so his senior cavalry officer, stated that the brigade numbered around 800 men, and this seems a more reliable estimate. Towards the end of March 1644 a London newsbook reported that 500 infantry and 300 cavalry had been recruited for Myddelton in and around London, and when on campaign the brigade never seems to have been much larger than this.[3] As well as the small regiments of horse, foot and dragoons that Myddelton had raised as a sergeant-major-general with a colonel's commission, his brigade included a regiment of foot commanded by his cousin Sir William Myddelton. In March 1644 Sir Thomas had agreed to

---

1   *The Perfect Occurrences of Parliament And Chief Collections of Letters*, 6-13 Sept. 1644.
2   NLW, Chirk Castle Manuscripts 1/Biii, 93, unfoliated.
3   *A Perfect Diurnall of some passages in Parliament*, 25 Mar.-1 Apr. 1644.

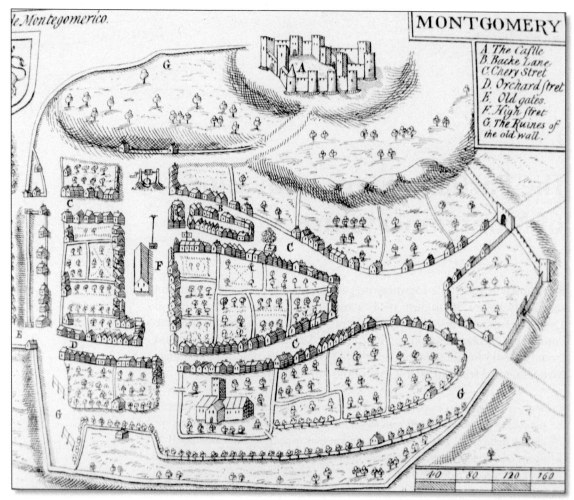

le Montegomerico.

MONTGOMERY

A The Castle
B Backe Lane
C Chery Stret
D Orchard stret
E Old gates.
F High stret
G The Ruines of
the old wall.

An early seventeenth-century plan of the town of Montgomery. It includes at the top the only known depiction of the castle, as it appeared before Lord Herbert's 1620s modernisation.

bankroll the raising of this ostensibly 500-strong regiment, by providing 'the arms, halberds, partisans, drums and colours', plus an initial advance of the wages for each soldier of six shillings and eight pence.[4]

Myddelton's Brigade marched from Oswestry during the afternoon of Tuesday 3 September. The immediate objectives of his offensive into Montgomeryshire were twofold, the second phase of the operation largely dependent on the success of the first. This would be an opportunistic attack, to fall upon the Royalists at Newtown with the aim of seizing a Chester-bound munitions convoy. Myddelton's second target and his main objective was to secure a stronghold in Montgomeryshire by gaining Montgomery Castle, the seat and home of Lord Herbert of Cherbury.[5]

---

4 NLW, Chirk Castle F Manuscripts, folio 6428.

5 The following reconstruction of the opening of Myddelton's campaign is based mainly on the correspondence of the Royalists Colonel Richard Herbert and Sir Michael Woodhouse in the British Library Additional (BL) Manuscripts 18981, Prince Rupert's Papers, respectively folios 242 and 245, and on two dispatches written by Sir Thomas Myddelton from Montgomery on 5 September, one to the Committee of Both Kingdoms, the other to his cousin, the recorder of London, John Glyn, published respectively in Historical Manuscripts Commission [hereafter HMC] *Fifth Report, Part I, Report and*

Newtown stood on a low promontory within a loop of the river Severn in the river's upper valley, and after Welshpool and Montgomery was the third most important of Montgomeryshire's market towns. It lay on the Chester to Cardiff road, which crossed the Severn via a timber bridge at the north end of the town's main street. Events had touched Newtown in 1642, but it was not until Oswestry fell to the Parliamentarians in

A scale model representing Montgomery Castle as it probably looked when completed in the later thirteenth century. The castle's strongly defended inner ward is to the right of the picture. (Courtesy of the Old Bell Museum, Montgomery)

June 1644 that the town assumed strategic importance. Oswestry allowed the Parliamentarians to increase the range at which they might interdict enemy convoys heading for Chester, causing the Royalists to route their supply line further west into Wales.

Since their capture of Bristol in July 1643, the city and port had become a vital depot for the Royalists, especially to receive military supplies imported from the continent. Around mid-August 1644 a munitions convoy left Bristol carrying a supply of gunpowder to replenish the magazines at Shrewsbury and Chester. Having been ferried across the Severn estuary north of Bristol from Beachley Head to the landing on the Welsh side at St. Aust near Chepstow, the convoy had travelled the borderland north though Monmouthshire and Herefordshire reaching Hereford. From Hereford it crossed into south Shropshire to Ludlow, where the Royalist military governor, Sir Michael Woodhouse, detached some of his soldiers to escort the convoy on its westerly diversion to Newtown. There it would cross the Severn and continue northward on the Chester road, via the Royalist staging post at Chirk Castle in Denbighshire. Newtown at the time was occupied by Captain Gardiner's troop of Prince Rupert's Regiment of Horse, and two other troops were billeted not far from the town. The convoy seems to have arrived at Newtown during 3 September, the day Myddelton's Brigade marched from Oswestry.

The importance of acting upon good intelligence came into play at this point. According to Sir Michael Woodhouse, although Gardiner received news forewarning him 'that the enemy had a desire upon him', he failed to concentrate all three troops of horse in Newtown. Myddelton, on the other hand, as he had in raiding Welshpool, made effective use of intelligence to discover Gardiner's dispositions. 'Understanding the motions of the enemy, and which way they were designed, and what their strength was', according to one of his officers, gave Myddelton an advantage at the outset of the

---

Appendix (London 1876), p. 27, and *A Perfect Diurnall of some passages in Parliament*, 9 Sept. 1644.

Edward, first Baron Herbert of Cherbury (portrayed as a younger man). The battle was fought as a result of Lord Herbert's surrender of his home at Montgomery Castle to Parliamentary forces. (Private collection, courtesy of Rhian Davies

campaign. His chief informer, or 'intelligencer', seems to have been one Piers David, who at one point was paid a gratuity by Myddelton worth almost £21 for spying in Montgomeryshire – a substantial lump sum, equivalent to about two years' good wages for an unskilled labourer.[6]

Having advanced quickly southward by forced marches through the night of 3/4 September, Wednesday morning found Myddelton's Brigade some way south of Welshpool on the Severn's west bank. Because little is known about the roads and river crossings in seventeenth-century Montgomeryshire, Myddelton's route cannot be re-constructed with any confidence. However, not far from the Red Castle the brigade encountered the only resistance during its march: 'no enemy appearing', Myddelton noted, 'saving some horse which issued out of the Red Castle, the Lord Powis's house, whereof we slew one'. The way from Oswestry was arduous as a result of recent wet weather and enemy activity. The roadways were mired, and because the Royalists had broken some bridges the Parliamentarians had to use fords made treacherous by the high level of the watercourses.

Although the sources on this point are contradictory, it appears that Myddelton now divided his force. Most of the cavalry and dragoons, so upwards of 250 men, under the command of Lieutenant-colonel Till were detached to Newtown to seize the convoy, while Myddelton awaited the outcome with his own troop, a few dragoons and all the infantry.

Till's force marched rapidly to Newtown later on Wednesday morning and soon attacked. While his tactical plan will remain unknown, Till clearly took the enemy by surprise. The Royalist picquets were overwhelmed, and the main guard, the small reserve on duty in town, soon surrendered. There were few casualties on either side, and the Parliamentarians reported the capture of Gardiner, two junior officers and about 40 troopers, along with two troop colours. The remaining Royalists fled. The Parliamentarians captured 36 barrels of gunpowder, 12 barrels of sulphur (an ingredient of gunpowder that could only be sourced overseas), stocks of match and bullets and a quantity of weaponry, along with the convoy's four wagons. The loss of the sulphur was especially damaging for the Royalists because it was urgently needed to maintain the production of the gunpowder mill at Chester; which, as Myddelton crowed in his report to London, 'cannot be supplied with for any money in those parts'.

Upon receiving news of Till's success, Myddelton resumed the march eastward to Montgomery where most of the brigade arrived during Wednesday afternoon, having crossed the Severn by the bridge at Caerhowel.

---

6   *A Diary, or an Exact Journal*, 13 Sept. 1644; The National Archives (TNA), SP28/346 Part 1, unfoliated.

On approaching and entering Montgomery the Parliamentarians met no opposition from the few Royalist soldiers said to have been remaining in the area, and Myddelton made Richard Herbert's town house his own headquarters.

Myddelton's objective now was to secure Montgomery Castle. It was sited overlooking Montgomery on a defensible narrow rocky ridge, running north to south and precipitous at its northern end, that outcropped from the hill county rising immediately east of the town. At the time of the Civil Wars late medieval castles could still make effective bases, and many were garrisoned throughout England and Wales. Even castles that had become disused and fallen into disrepair were often made into habitable and defensible strongholds.

Montgomery Castle had been constructed during the first half of the thirteenth century as an important stronghold of the English crown on the contested borderland of Wales. It had originally comprised three wards, or walled enclosures. The strongest was the northerly inner ward, dominated on the west side by the great well tower and with a twin-towered gatehouse that defended the crossing of the rock cut ditch separating it from the middle ward. Most of the later modifications to the medieval fortress had been made to this middle ward. Here, a range of sixteenth century lodgings had been demolished and replaced in 1622-5 with a fine L-shaped mansion in two wings built by Lord Herbert. Copying the latest architectural styles, Herbert's residence was built mostly of brick. However, the mansion's gated main entrance passage was still defended by a drawbridge crossing the outer rock cut ditch. Although Herbert had invested most heavily in the construction of his mansion, known as 'the New Building', the medieval fabric of 'the Old Castle' had been kept in good repair and it was defensible at the time of the Civil War. The less substantial perimeter wall of the castle's outer ward at the southern end of the ridge, however, by 1644 seems to have been completely ruinous or even demolished and cleared away.

In its place Herbert had had constructed a defensive earthen outwork commanding the approach to the middle ward and mansion. Described as comprising 'of two banks', this may have been a ravelin – a ditched and embanked defence with two faces forming a salient angle. Herbert's mansion had weakened the castle's defences, necessitating the building of this covering outwork. As Richard Herbert pointed out in January 1649 to Parliamentary commissioners, in the hope of saving the mansion when the entire castle was threatened with demolition, 'you would be pleased to certify how weak a structure that of the New Building is, being built after the modern fashion of brick'. Nonetheless, in September 1644 Montgomery Castle remained a formidable stronghold. The experienced soldier Sir John Meldrum reckoned it was 'one of the goodliest and strongest places that ever I looked upon'.

Lord Herbert's building of the defensive outwork raises questions of his allegiance, and whether he had garrisoned the castle. Historians have tended to dismiss Herbert as an eccentric recluse. However, he merits more balanced consideration because the battle of Montgomery resulted from his actions.

About sixty-two years of age in 1644, vain and somewhat conceited, but by then in poor health, Herbert had led a most active life. As a younger man he had spent considerable time on the Continent, as a traveller and in soldiering as a gentleman volunteer. Based on this experience he became a diplomat, as the English ambassador to France during the latter part of the reign of King James I. As a somewhat peripheral courtier during the reign of Charles I, Herbert turned successfully to writing, becoming a respected philosopher, historian and poet. However, like many other peers Herbert in 1639-40 had faithfully rallied to King Charles during the so-called Bishops' Wars against the Covenanter regime in Scotland. He had sought a military command in 1639, while during 1640, in April in the House of Lords, and in October at the Great Council of peers held at York, he advocated the prosecution of military operations against the rebel Scots. During 1641 Herbert attended court more often, and in the factious political climate from November onwards sat regularly in the Lords among a group of peers supportive of the King. After Charles abandoned London in January, politicised opinion in London turned increasingly aggressively against his supporters in Parliament. Consequently, in March 1642 Herbert returned to Montgomery.[7]

That summer King Charles appointed Herbert to the commissions of array for Montgomeryshire and Shropshire. It is unclear how active a Royalist Herbert was, but he probably backed and bankrolled his son Richard's recruitment drive. Lord Herbert did not attend the Royalist parliament convened at Oxford in January 1644, and a month later claimed ill health as the reason for not attending on Prince Rupert when he arrived in Shropshire. He furthermore respectfully but firmly rebutted the Prince's plan to place a regular garrison in Montgomery Castle. Herbert pointed out that soldiers of Richard's regiment were then billeted in the town, and that in any case he could always gather a sufficient garrison from among his servants, tenants and other followers. Towards the end of September 1644, three members of his household signed an affidavit mentioning that Herbert had indeed planned to call up an ad-hoc local militia up to 150 strong to defend the castle. However, Herbert did consent to Prince Rupert sending up to 60 regular soldiers to Montgomery, providing that he could nominate the officers, that they would be under his command, and that, apart from a guard camped in the castle's outwork, the soldiers would be billeted in the town.

The Prince's policy elsewhere was to put professional soldiers in charge of garrisons, in place of local grandees and gentleman officers with little or no previous military experience. However, perhaps out of deference to Herbert's status as a respected peer of the realm Rupert did not force the issue, despite Richard Herbert pressing his own candidacy for the governorship of Montgomery Castle.[8] Richard seems to have reckoned, rightly as events turned out, that is father's increasingly hesitant Royalism, coupled to what does seem to have been a genuine marked decline in his health, might leave the castle worryingly exposed in his charge. However, in April Prince Rupert instead posted Richard to the coast of mid west-Wales as governor of

7   D.A. Palin, 'Edward Herbert, first Baron Herbert of Cherbury (1582?–1648)', *Oxford Dictionary of National Biography* [hereafter *ODNB*] (40 vols., Oxford, 2004), Vol. 26, pp. 663-8; R. Cust, *Charles I And The Aristocracy, 1625-1642* (Cambridge, 2013), pp. 185, 206-7, 252, 319.

8   Warburton, *Prince Rupert and the Cavaliers*, Vol. 1, p. 501.

Aberystwyth Castle. On 23 August Lord Herbert again cited ill health (he feared an eye condition might result in the loss of his sight) and his beginning a course of treatment in apologetic justification for not meeting with Rupert on his journey to Bristol.[9]

When Myddelton's Brigade occupied Montgomery almost a fortnight later, Richard Herbert, then at Ludlow in Shropshire, reckoned that his father had garrisoned the castle

The modern bridge crossing the ditch defending the middle ward of Montgomery Castle. There was a drawbridge here in 1644 at the entrance to Lord Herbert's mansion, which stood to the left of the photograph.

with about 30 men. There were some regular Royalist soldiers among them, including one Thomas Lloyd. He later claimed that having fought and been captured in Shropshire during 1643, after being released he was posted to Montgomery Castle, serving there 'until it was taken by the enemy'.[10] Furthermore, Lord Herbert later acknowledged that he had kept a private magazine at the castle, well stocked with pikes, muskets, gunpowder, two small brass cannon and a supply of lead for casting bullets.[11]

Outwardly, then, Lord Herbert held Montgomery Castle for the King, but he lacked both the commitment and the physical stamina to actively defend the place. Indeed, in justifying his actions to the House of Commons in March 1646, Herbert cited evidence that in August 1644 he had made preparations to settle his affairs at Montgomery with the intention of leaving for London, reasoning that he had more hope of finding treatment for his eye condition there than in Wales.[12] Herbert's actions were also swayed by the threatened confiscation of his London property. The sequestration of capital and assets of known or suspected Royalists was commonly authorised by Parliament, and on 9 February 1644 orders had been issued for Herbert's goods to be seized and sold to fund Parliamentary forces. Herbert's treasured library was included, and on 30 August the Commons gave particular orders for this to be auctioned. However, on 21 September, before the outcome of events at Montgomery was known in London, the House of Lords ordered a stay on any further sale or disposal of Herbert's goods, 'until testimony given of his Lordship's behaviour touching his character and demeanour to the Parliament and their proceedings'. When certain reports of the victory at Montgomery were announced in Parliament on the 23rd, the

9   BL, Additional Manuscripts 18981, folios 67, 242.
10 NLW, Chirk Castle Manuscripts, B86, maimed soldier petitions, folio 132.
11 NLW, Herbert Manuscripts and Papers, Series II, Vol. IX, E6/1, folio 37.
12 Ibid., E6/1, folio 14.

Lords and Commons the same day jointly ordered the lifting of Herbert's sequestration. His remaining goods and books were to be kept for return to him.[13] This raises the question whether Herbert had beforehand entered into clandestine negotiations with Parliament to surrender Montgomery Castle. The Parliamentarians later denied this, but after the battle on 18 September Sir Thomas Myddelton had taken time to pen a favourable letter to the Lords and Commons, noting that Lord Herbert 'had done nothing that might justly offend the houses of Parliament'.[14]

While it seems that Myddelton expected to gain the castle without opposition, Herbert did not immediately surrender the place. Myddelton wrote to London from Montgomery on the morning of Thursday 5 September, that 'I have sent my Lord of Cherbury about the surrendering of the castle of Montgomery unto me for the Parliament's service […] and have received a very good and satisfactory answer from him'. Negotiations were conducted via Myddelton's intermediary Captain Samuel More, one of Colonel Mytton's officers of the Shropshire forces. While there is no evidence that any of Mytton's soldiers joined Myddelton's Brigade in Montgomeryshire, More seems to have acted as liaison officer between Myddelton and the Shropshire Parliamentarians. Samuel More and, until his death in December 1643, his late father Richard, a Shropshire MP, had been active Parliamentarians since 1642. Attached to Myddelton's Brigade Samuel may have hoped to use his familial influence in south-west Shropshire, bordering on Montgomeryshire, to gain support for Parliament there.

Negotiations between Myddelton and Herbert became increasingly awkward.[15] The latter may have thought it would be in his future interest to be able to demonstrate to his erstwhile fellow Royalists that he had at least put up as show of resistance; or perhaps he hoped that by stalling the actual or threatened arrival of Royalist forces would cause Myddelton to withdraw. Via More, Herbert offered Myddelton a cash bribe; either to withdraw from Montgomery, or not to assault and plunder the castle, depending on how the sources are interpreted. For their part, the Parliamentarians expected to be allowed to occupy the castle's outworks so that the munitions captured at Newtown could be kept there overnight, and for security that Herbert would dismiss most of his garrison. Herbert objected to this condition, but was given until 9.00 am on Friday morning to reach a decision.

Notwithstanding this agreement, around 7.00 pm on Thursday evening the Parliamentarians went ahead and occupied the castle outworks, probably because of the arrival from Newtown of Lieutenant-colonel Till with the munitions. As the evening drew on, Myddelton would have been increasingly mindful that with the castle still ostensibly in enemy hands, and with the likelihood of the arrival in the area of Royalist forces, that his situation at

---

13   *Journals of the House of Commons*, Vol. 3, pp. 612, 394; *Journals of the House of Lords*, Vol. 6, pp. 712-13.

14   NLW, Herbert Manuscripts and Papers, Series II, Vol. IX, E6/1, folio 5.

15   The following reconstruction of events is based ˌ ly on NLW, Herbert Manuscripts and Papers, Series II, Vol. IX, E6/1, folios   ˌ emented by Anon., 'Various Documents relating to Montgomery C   ˌ ', in *Collections Historical and Archaeological Relating to Montgomerysı   ˌ ers* (1881), pp. 181-3.

Montgomery was vulnerable. Accordingly, he ordered Till to force Herbert's surrender.

Around midnight, Till led a storming party equipped with a petard – a portable demolition charge – into the ditch before the middle ward below the raised drawbridge. Climbing a ladder, they prised some planks from the foot of the drawbridge and entered the mansion's entrance passage leading to the main gate: 'without any resistance of the guards, whom it seemed wanted will or courage to resist them'. Till formally summoned Herbert's attention by a trumpet call and demanded the immediate surrender of the castle. A verbal exchange ensued between the two men either side of the gate. Herbert demanded that Till withdraw on the grounds that the agreement to defer negotiations until later Friday morning had been broken, to which Till replied by threatening to attach the petard and blow in the gate. Clearly neither Herbert nor his followers had the stomach for a fight, and so he agreed to the inevitable capitulation. Till dictated the terms for the surrender of the castle agreed by Herbert in the small hours of the morning of Friday 6 September.

The terms were civil and generous. Herbert and his daughter Beatrice, who was with him at the time, with up to ten servants were allowed to remain in the castle with private use of their personal apartments and possessions. Herbert's study and library in particular were to remain sacrosanct. Should the Herberts wish to leave with their portable possessions, they would have a military escort as far as Coventry in Warwickshire. Herbert's chattels, livestock and provisions would not be seized, and arrangements were made for the continued management of his landed estate around Montgomery. The Parliamentarians required two rooms for bedchambers, one for Myddelton the other for the governor, and lodgings for a permanent garrison of 20 soldiers. The Parliamentarians probably occupied the castle around daybreak, and Myddelton appointed Captain More as governor.

4

The Royalist counter-attack and the widening campaign

While the capitulation of Montgomery Castle was still being decided, the Royalists in Shropshire were already preparing to launch a counter-attack.[1]

By the early afternoon of Thursday 5 September, Colonel Richard Herbert, then at Ludlow, 30 miles south-east of Montgomery by modern roads, knew that Myddelton had occupied Montgomery with about 600 men (although it had also been erroneously reported that a larger Parliamentary force was threatening the Red Castle). Meanwhile, at a council of war held at or near Shrewsbury, the area commander Sir Michael Ernle, together with Sir Michael Woodhouse and Sir Lewis Kirke (the governor of the main Royalist garrison in east Shropshire at Bridgnorth), had agreed to despatch forces to relieve Lord Herbert who was expected to make some attempt to hold out at Montgomery. Once Herbert's capitulation was known, the Royalists remained determined to attack before the Parliamentarians had time to gather provisions and improve the defences of Montgomery, and to prevent them from fortifying Newtown. The area had now assumed strategic importance. Richard Herbert reckoned that the town and fertile vale of Montgomery would allow the Parliamentarians to maintain a substantial cavalry force there. The Royalists also intended to regain the vital munitions lost at Newtown.

Sir Michael Ernle intended to send up to 1,100 foot and 1,400 horse into Montgomeryshire. Although the size of force actually deployed is unknown, the Royalists substantially outnumbered Myddelton's Brigade. The infantry were drawn from the Shropshire garrisons, while the cavalry comprised Sir William Vaughan's Regiment, the remaining troops of Prince Rupert's Regiment – by then withdrawn into south Shropshire after the recent defeats in Montgomeryshire – and a body of Northern Horse, who since their defeat at Malpas had retreated into Shropshire. Ernle hoped that the Northern Horse

---

1   Main sources for the Royalist response are the dispatches to Prince Rupert by officers involved: BDL, Firth Manuscripts C7, folio 167, Richard Herbert (7 Sept. 1644); BL, Additional Manuscripts 18981, folios 242, 245, 253 – respectively, Richard Herbert (5 Sept. 1644), Sir Michael Woodhouse (5 Sept. 1644), Sir Michael Ernle (19 Sept. 1644). The lost Mostyn family manuscript cited by Parry in *Royal Visits and Progresses to Wales*, p. 386, provides additional information.

Caus Castle, Shropshire. The fragmentary remains of the western gateway of the late medieval town that stood here until the mid sixteenth century. On 6-7 September 1644 Caus was the mustering point for Royalist forces directed against Montgomery.

would form at least half of the expeditionary force's cavalry. On 4 September Ernle had requested of their acting commanding officer Major Samuel Tuke, in charge in the wounded Langdale's absence, that his horsemen should be deployed against Myddelton in Montgomeryshire. Although Tuke at first had flatly refused to cooperate, citing Prince Rupert's orders to continue the southerly march, he later relented and part of the division about-turned and marched back through Ludlow.

They went on to join the rendezvous of Ernle's forces planned to take place from the afternoon of Friday 6 September at Caus Castle, about ten miles south-west of Shrewsbury and the same distance to Montgomery. Sited on an upland area stretching to the Welsh border known as the Long Mountain, the strong, originally thirteenth century stone-built castle at Caus had been owned since the 1590s and extensively modernised by the Thyne family. In 1644 the castle was the usual residence of Sir Henry Thyne, a Royalist. He probably maintained a small garrison there along the lines of a personal retinue, although a larger force of regulars would be posted to Caus after the battle of Montgomery. The castle stood within a large earthwork enclosure, the modified ditches and ramparts of a prehistoric hill fort, which had defended the late medieval borough at Caus. This enclosure would have provided a muster point and camping ground for the gathering Royalist forces.

The Royalists attacked Montgomery early on 8 September. The horse were commanded by Vaughan and Sir Thomas Dallison and the foot by Colonel Robert Broughton, the governor of Shrewsbury. Advancing from Caus, they appear to have divided to approach Montgomery from two directions, from

The rampart and accompanying ditch of a surviving stretch of Montgomery's late medieval defences. A surmounting circuit of town walls and towers may never have been fully completed, and along with the town gates was in disrepair or ruinous by the seventeenth century. These defences do not seem to have played much part in the fighting during September 1644.

the north crossing the river Camlad and from the north-east via Chirbury. The Parliamentarians were not wholly taken by surprise, and made some attempt to defend the approaches to the town in skirmishing which slowed the Royalist advance, allowing Myddelton's foot to withdraw into the castle. With most of his horse and dragoons Myddelton fled northwards pursed by Royalist cavalry, although he was almost captured when the Royalists caught up with them crossing a bridge. During this pursuit the Royalists took more than 30 Parliamentarians prisoner, but Myddelton and most of his men made good their escape to Oswestry.

With the arrival of the main body of foot under Broughton the Royalists set about laying siege to Montgomery Castle. Little is known about the course of the siege over the following ten days. To cordon off the castle and as besieging positions the Royalists raised earthworks, presumably sited at the southern end of the castle ridge and on the hill slopes to the west, but no certain trace of these has been found. The plough-flattened remains of the ditch and bank of a rectangular enclosure on low ground a couple of hundred yards due north of the castle may be the remains of a small Royalist fortlet or redoubt, built to prevent forays by the garrison in that direction, but again the archaeological evidence is unproven. The substantial earthworks of the prehistoric hill fort crowning the summit of Fridd Faldwyn, overlooking the castle a few hundred yards to the north-west, would have provided the Royalists with a ready-made encampment. Closer to the castle ran the ditch and rampart of the western stretch of the late medieval town defences. This earthwork remains a substantial feature in the landscape today, and could have been held by the Royalists as an approach, or advanced position.

The thirteenth-century earthwork remains of Montgomery's westerly defences. In September 1644 either Royalists or Parliamentarians may have occupied this position during the ten-day siege of the castle, seen in the background.

Alternatively, the Parliamentarians may have occupied it to conduct an aggressive forward defence.

The reportedly large number of unrecorded finds of musket balls discovered by treasure hunters metal detecting during the 1980s and 1990s in the fields below Fridd Faldwyn attest to the Royalist besiegers being exposed to musketry and sniping fire from the castle's defenders.[2] That the sizeable garrison numbering 400-500 men under the command of Lieutenant-colonel Till and Captain More conducted an active defence is indicated by Sir Thomas Myddelton's later remark, that on the Sunday before the battle, 15 September, the Royalists wounded in the siege so far were evacuated from Montgomery to Shrewsbury by a convoy of 14 carts.[3]

Notwithstanding their defiant defence, the garrison was isolated with no immediate hope of relief in what remained ostensibly enemy territory. Containment, then, was the priority of the Royalist besiegers under the command of Colonel Broughton. Starving the Parliamentarians into surrender was a foreseeable outcome, for they had not had time since occupying Montgomery to stockpile sufficient supplies to feed so many for any length of time. As Myddelton later acknowledged, 'the enemy hastened to come upon us before we could bring in provisions for our garrison'. Perhaps for this reason, and in respect for Lord Herbert, who with his daughter remained in the castle, and whose actions in surrendering the place would not have been fully know to them, the Royalists do not seem to

---

2   Walters and Hunnisett, *The Civil War Battlefield at Montgomery*, p. 2.
3   *CSPD, 1644*, p. 533.

Moreton Corbet Castle, Shropshire, an important Royalist garrison stormed and taken by Parliamentarians on 8 September 1644. This view shows the castle's impressive Elizabethan south range.

have assaulted the castle, and there is no evidence that they deployed siege artillery against it.

Meanwhile in Shropshire, on 8 September the Parliamentarians based at Wem had taken advantage of the Royalist preoccupation with events in Montgomeryshire by capturing the important garrison at Moreton Corbet Castle, strategically situated midway between Shrewsbury and Wem. It was taken by a small assault force of about 150 men, comprising dismounted Shropshire Horse and advance detachments from three companies of Cheshire Foot that Sir William Brereton was sending to Wem as reinforcements. They stormed the castle's outer earthworks and engaged in a short but fierce fire-fight, using hand grenades to dislodge the garrison from the buildings. Brereton reported more than 70 prisoners taken, two horse colours and a haul of military supplies. The loss of this key outpost covering Shrewsbury was another worrying setback for the Royalists.[4]

Sir Thomas Myddelton in the meantime, as he put it, 'hastened into Cheshire to procure relief'. He either met with or sent messages to Sir William Brereton at his forward based at Tarvin, where on 9 September he was overseeing its fortification, and gained his support. Sir John Meldrum, who was then either at the leaguer before Liverpool or at Manchester, the headquarters of the Lancashire Parliamentarians, also agreed to join forces to go to Myddelton's aid. Both Meldrum and Brereton recognised the strategic potential of Montgomery Castle as a bridgehead for further operations into Wales, while its loss would strike a humiliating and possibly irrevocably damaging blow to Myddelton's war effort and reputation. It also seems that their mutual respect at this time fostered a spirit of cooperation between the

---

4   Ibid., pp. 484-5.

three Parliamentarian regional commanders. As Meldrum reasoned to the Committee of Both Kingdoms:

> I was, by the earnest invitations of Sir William Brereton and Sir Thomas
> Myddelton, easily persuaded to concur with them for the relief of Montgomery
> Castle, besieged by the King's forces. I resolved to contribute my best endeavours
> in that expedition, as well in regard of the importance of the service, as that
> Liverpool was not to be attempted suddenly by such forces as I had.

Once events in Montgomeryshire were known in London, on 14 September the Committee of Both Kingdoms hastened belated orders to Sir William Brereton and the Parliamentarian county committees in Shropshire and Lancashire to commit forces and supplies to Myddelton's support. However, by that time regional Parliamentary forces were already gathering to march to the relief of Myddelton's beleaguered garrison at Montgomery. Reporting news filtering to the King's headquarters, at Oxford the Royalist journal *Mercurius Aulicus* acknowledged the significance of the developing campaign, for Royalist reinforcements under Lord Byron's command, drawn from Chester and north-east Wales, were now also heading for Montgomery: 'As for the siege of Liverpool, 'tis quite raised, the rebels under Brereton and Meldrum gone all thence with all that they can rake from the towns of Manchester, Wem, Nantwich & [etc.] to the relief of Montgomery Castle'.[5]

---

5   *CSPD, 1644*, p. 505; *Mercurius Aulicus*, 21 Sept. 1644.

5

The commanders

The Montgomery campaign reflected the diversity of military talent among the senior leaderships of the armies of the First English Civil War. It involved career soldiers, who before 1642 had led a predominantly military life, serving alongside officers of narrower experience, gentlemen for whom military practice in some form had been part and parcel of the wider accomplishments of their usually civilian lives. Given individual aptitude and the opportunity, then both groups became as much professional soldiers. As the Royalist captain of horse Richard Atkyns, a military novice himself in 1642, pointed out, the high tempo of the fighting provided ample occasion to develop military skill: 'which gave me more proficiency as a soldier in half a year's time, than generally in the Low Countries in four or five years'.[1] Atkyns's experience serves to reinforce Peter Newman's argument, that 'it takes little wit to perceive that within a short time the King's commanders, and those of Parliament, became real soldiers if they were not already so'.[2]

The Parliamentarians

To first consider the leadership of the Parliamentarian army at Montgomery, his fellow senior commanders Sir William Brereton and Sir Thomas Myddelton jointly agreed to **Sir John Meldrum** (*b.* before 1584, *d.* 1645) taking overall command. This showed an impressive unanimity of purpose, for Brereton, and especially Myddelton (as Parliament's sergeant-major-general for North Wales) both outranked Meldrum, had greater regional interests and more at stake in the outcome of the campaign. However, both would have respected the experience and repute of the probably sixty-year-old Scots veteran. As Brereton acknowledged in his post-battle dispatch to London: 'Sir John Meldrum did with much judgement order and command these forces, and therefore deserves a large share in the honour of this day's success'.

Meldrum was a notable example of the many Scots officers who, having campaigned on the Continent during the 1620s and 1630s as mercenaries

1 R. Atkyns, *The Vindication of Richard Atkyns, Esquire* (London, 1669), p. 19.
2 P.R. Newman, *The Old Service: Royalist Regimental Colonels and the Civil War, 1642-46* (Manchester, 1993), p. 10.

in the Thirty Years War, in 1642 provided an influx of professional military talent to the armies of King and Parliament. Of obscure origins, Meldrum hitherto had also dutifully served the Stuart Crown. In justifying his opposition to King Charles I, in October 1642 Meldrum wrote of 'the zeal I had in your majesty's father's service in Ireland, settling the province of Ulster, and in your own service at Rochelle'; referring to his time soldiering in Ireland during the reign of King James I, and to taking part in 1627 in the ill-fated amphibious operations by English forces at Ile de Ré during the Anglo-French conflict of 1627-9. By 1632 Meldrum was colonel of a regiment of foot in Prussia, like many thousands of fellow Scots, officers and rank and file, having taken employment in the Protestant army of Gustav II Adolph, King of Sweden.

In 1642 Meldrum sided with Parliament and would be employed in several roles, leading his biographer aptly to describe him as a military 'trouble-shooter'.[3] That spring and into summer Meldrum was in east Yorkshire vigorously organising the defence of Hull, a key arsenal and important port, before transferring to the south coast to assist in the capture of Portsmouth. He was one of several high-ranking Scots in the Earl of Essex's Army and fought as a regimental and brigade commander of foot at the battle of Edgehill. Meldrum returned north in 1643, and in June was appointed operational commander of the Parliamentary military association of East Midland counties headed by Lord Grey of Groby. As one London journal approvingly commented on his appointment:

Sir John Meldrum was commander-in-chief of the Parliamentarian army at Montgomery.

> [The Earl of Essex] to take away all the differences between the commanders on the counties of Lincoln, Leicester and Nottingham hath sent Sir John Meldrum, a Scottish man, to command in chief. This noble gentleman hath hitherto showed himself faithful and valiant in the Parliament's and kingdom's cause, his valour and fidelity hath been thoroughly testified, at Portsmouth, Hull and Edgehill, and in other places.[4]

Remaining in this regional theatre of the war, Meldrum in July joined with Colonel Oliver Cromwell in the operations around Gainsborough (Lincolnshire), and returning to Hull, in October led the counter attack that broke the second Royalist siege.

In late February 1644, Meldrum assisted by Lord Willoughby of Parham, commanding in Lincolnshire, with the East Midlands forces beleaguered the strategically important Royalist stronghold of Newark (Nottinghamshire). However, on 21 March Meldrum's besieging army numbering 6,000-7,000 men was out-manoeuvred and partially defeated by a Royalist relief force led by Prince Rupert and so capitulated the next day. The Parliamentarian soldiers were allowed to march away, but with the humiliating surrender

---

3   C. Carlton, 'Meldrum, Sir John (b. before 1584?, d. 1645)', *ODNB*, Vol. 37, pp. 739-40.
4   *Certaine Informations from Several Parts of the Kingdom*, 19-26 June 1643.

of their arms, artillery and military supplies. The relief of Newark was a demoralising setback to the regional Parliamentarians and Meldrum's first notable defeat. Robert Baillie was a well-informed Presbyterian minister with the Scots delegation in London of the Solemn League and Covenant. Baillie's reporting seems to have reflected informed opinion within the Scots-Parliamentarian alliance, and (prophetically as events turned out) he had earlier pointed to what was perceived to be Meldrum's stubborn misjudgment in besieging Newark: 'Though his error be palpable, yet he is so tender of his reputation, that he will not rise, though there be no hope in carrying it; yea, it is likely to draw Prince Rupert with a great strength upon him'. After receiving on 24 March the news of the defeat at Newark, Baillie wrote ruefully: 'Sir John Meldrum by all means would besiege Newark, and gave assurance to all, day after day, to carry it; yet it is so fallen out, whether by base cowardice or treachery, that his whole camp […] after a little skirmish, has rendered themselves to the enemy […] a grievous and disgraceful stroke'.[5]

On the following 12 April Meldrum led a division of foot of the Fairfax's Northern Army in the assault on Selby (Yorkshire), an important regional Parliamentary victory which threatened the Royalist position in northern England. It also helped Meldrum to reconsolidate his reputation. In later May Meldrum was again entrusted with an independent command, when, with two regiments of foot and some horse, he was sent from the Allied army besieging Royalist York under orders from the Committee of Both Kingdoms to shore up the Parliamentarian cause in Lancashire, in disarray since Prince Rupert's advance into the county earlier that month. Meldrum had specific instructions to hold Manchester, where he arrived on 28 May.[6] He stabilised the situation of the Lancashire Parliamentarians, and as a consequence of the battle of Marston Moor, by August Meldrum was in a position to act against Royalist forces remaining in Lancashire under Lord Byron's command. The retreat into Lancashire of the Northern Horse complicated Meldrum's task, but, as has been seen, he defeated and scattered Langdale's and Byron's forces at Ormskirk on 20 August. With inland Lancashire cleared of Royalists apart from a couple of isolated garrisons, Meldrum turned his attention to capturing the port of Liverpool, which he had begun closely to invest by early September.

While Meldrum was clearly the proficient seasoned campaigner (his recent success in Lancashire most likely dispelling any remaining doubts about his suitability for independent high command stemming from the humiliating defeat outside Newark) and his well-deserved repute made him a fitting choice to command-in-chief at Montgomery, by autumn 1644 both of his fellow commanders had become capable soldiers.

There is, however, no evidence that either Sir Thomas Myddelton or Sir William Brereton had undertaken active service before 1642, although both would have gained some experience from their pre-war military duties as deputies to the lord lieutenant in their home counties of Denbighshire and Cheshire respectively. A deputy lieutenancy in Stuart England and Wales has been described as being 'the pinnacle in the hierarchy of county offices', and

---

5   Anon., *The Letters and Journals of Robert Baillie* (Edinburgh, 1841), Vol. 2, pp. 156, 158.
6   *CSPD, 1644*, pp. 173, 191, 206.

for Myddelton and Brereton reflected their status as notable titled members of the gentry class, with Myddelton being the wealthier of the two.[7] Both were landowners and businessmen (Brereton being especially entrepreneurial), and in 1642 were also serving magistrates and members of Parliament for their respective counties.

Sir Thomas Myddelton (*b.* 1586, *d.* 1666) was an unlikely belligerent Parliamentarian. In religious matters, frequently the main principled reason for taking up arms on either side, he was a loyal, moderate Anglican and politically a constitutional royalist. His militancy seem to have sprung from a fear of militant Catholicism and his distrust of the persona of King Charles I.[8] The seizure by local Royalists in January 1643 of Myddelton's home and estate at Chirk Castle propelled him into an unfamiliar militarily active role. He owed his appointment that June as Parliament's sergeant-major-general for North Wales for being the leading native Parliamentarian in a region that was solidly Royalist. In his later fifties Myddelton was old for an untried general, but he campaigned actively, in summer 1644, before the Montgomery campaign, in Staffordshire and Shropshire, and had established a working relationship with Brereton during their joint campaigns of autumn 1643. Leading his brigade into Montgomeryshire in early September 1644 was, however, Myddelton's first independent command.

Sir William Brereton (*b.* 1604, *d.* 1661) of Handforth, Cheshire, can fairly be characterised as a determined Puritan – 'a Protestant nationalist with marked anti-Catholic views' – and his active opposition to Charles I was probably grounded in religious scruple.[9] In summer 1642 Brereton had attempted to create a Parliamentarian party and to seize the initiative in Cheshire. Nonetheless, he had been unable to secure the city of Chester for Parliament, and when the Royalists gained ascendancy in the region Brereton retired to London. In December neutralists among Cheshire's divided gentry had engineered a cease-fire, disadvantaging the Chester-based Royalists, but this collapsed quickly when in later January 1643 Brereton returned from London bringing military supplies and leading around 500 horse and dragoons. Joining forces with upwards of 2,000 volunteers under local gentry leadership, Brereton set about clearing eastern and southern Cheshire of Royalists. He garrisoned the main towns including Nantwich which he made his headquarters, having beaten the forces of Sir Thomas Aston, his leading local Royalist opponent, from there on 28 January, and secured further local victories at Tarporley, 21 February, and at Middlewich, 13 March. Notwithstanding frequent enemy counter attacks and incursions, apart from Chester and its surrounding westerly districts Brereton would maintain control over most of Cheshire throughout the war.

On 25 March 1643 Brereton was appointed commander-in-chief of Parliament's Cheshire forces, and later engrossed further powers to enable him to prosecute the war as the undisputed military and political county

---

7 A. Fletcher, *Reform in the Provinces, The Government of Stuart England* (New Haven and London, 1986), p. 297.

8 J.G. Williams, 'Myddelton, Sir Thomas (1586–1666)', *ODNB*, Vol. 40, pp. 53-4.

9 J. Morrill, 'Sir William Brereton and England's Wars of Religion', *The Journal of British Studies* (1985), p. 313.

boss. Brereton was the energetic driving force of the Parliamentarian war effort in Cheshire until the First Civil War ended there with the achievement in early February 1646 of his main objective since summer 1642, the taking of Chester. Brereton had also pursued broader regional strategic objectives, as his biographer has pointed out: 'He waged an aggressive and relentless war throughout the north Midlands. At different times he took his troops into each of the seven counties that are contiguous with Cheshire and led joint operations with local commanders there'.[10] The Montgomery campaign was a notable case in point.

Subordinate to Sir John Meldrum and his assistant generals Myddelton and Brereton, the two other most senior officers of the Parliamentarian army were the major-generals of horse and foot. Their particular duty on campaign and especially on the day of battle was to oversee the deployment and tactical handling of the cavalry and infantry respectively.

Major-general of the combined Parliamentarian horse was **Colonel Sir William Fairfax** (*bap.* 1610, *d.* 1644), who by his death from multiple wounds after the battle became a posthumous hero, idolised in the Parliamentary London press. Typically, the *Scottish Dove* reported on 27 September 1644 how: 'Sir William Fairfax received many wounds in the fight […] such was his zeal to the cause, preferring the advantage of the day above his life; he was a man [worth] many thousands and his loss [is] to be lamented'.

At the outbreak of civil war Fairfax was a company captain in the Yorkshire trained bands, but as he raised a regiment of foot around London in August 1642 his previous military experience may have been more deeply grounded. Sir William was thus quickly militarily active in Parliament's cause while his uncle, Ferdinando, Lord Fairfax, and cousin, Ferdinando's son, Sir Thomas, who together became the driving force of Parliamentarianism in Yorkshire, were still refraining from taking up arms. Of Steeton Hall in the West Riding of Yorkshire, a region where popular Puritanism combined with anti-Catholicism generated strong support for Parliament, Sir William like other zealous Parliamentarians believed he was engaged in a religious war against the latent Roman Catholic, or Papist, followers of the King.[11] In writing to his wife while on campaign in November 1643, he expressed his motivation in stark terms: 'For Thomas's [Sir Thomas Fairfax] part and mine we rest neither night nor day, nor will willingly till we have done God some good service against his and our enemies'.[12]

Instead of returning to Yorkshire, in late September 1642 Sir William and his regiment were attached to the Earl of Essex's Army and fought in Sir John Meldrum's brigade at Edgehill. There the regiment fled and was mostly broken. Sir William later returned north and recruited a new regiment for Lord Fairfax's Northern Army. Given his experience hitherto as an infantry officer he commanded the foot at the capture of Wakefield (Yorkshire) in May 1643, but it was as a cavalry leader that he made his mark at the battle

10 J. Morrill, 'Brereton, Sir William, first Baronet (1604–1661)', *ODNB*, Vol. 7, pp. 471-3.
11 A.J. Hopper, 'Fairfax, Sir William (*bap.* 1610, *d.* 1644)', *ODND*, Vol. 5, p. 943; A.J. Hopper, *'Black Tom': Sir Thomas Fairfax and The English Revolution* (Manchester, 2007), pp. 26, 130-45, 157.
12 Markham, *Life of Robert Fairfax*, p. 14.

of Nantwich on 25 January 1644. Leading the Yorkshire Horse, probably including his own regiment, on difficult enclosed ground on the right wing of Sir Thomas Fairfax's army, Sir William provided vital support for the hard-pressed infantry in the centre. As Sir Thomas later acknowledged: 'The horse commanded by Sir William Fairfax did expose themselves to great danger, to encourage the foot, though capable of little service in those narrow lanes'.[13] Remaining with his cousin in the region, Sir William with several troops of Yorkshire Horse was beaten and routed at Market Drayton (Shropshire) by Prince Rupert on 5 March following.

Having suffered from a debilitating camp fever during April, in May Sir William had recovered and rejoined the Fairfax's forces with the Allied army in leaguer around York. He fought at Marston Moor, although it is uncertain whether in command of a brigade of Yorkshire Foot or of just his own regiment of horse. In later July Lord Fairfax sent Sir William in command of a task force of about 1,000 Yorkshire Horse to reinforce Sir John Meldrum's operations in Lancashire. Accordingly, in early September, on the eve of the Montgomery campaign, Sir William was preparing to lead his cavalry from the leaguer before Liverpool to clear the Wirral peninsula of any remaining Royalists.[14]

Fairfax's counterpart at Montgomery as major-general in charge of the Parliamentarian foot was **Major James Lothian** of Brereton's Cheshire army. Lothian was a Scottish professional soldier, although his earlier career is unknown. He was posted to Cheshire from London in later February 1643, in response to Brereton's urgent request to Parliament to be sent a sergeant-major of foot.[15] By all accounts Lothian seems to have been a thoroughly capable infantry officer and soon proved his worth. An account of the successful assault on Middlewich by Brereton's forces on 13 March 1643 described Lothian admiringly as 'our major (a right Scottish blade)', for his leading role with the foot in securing the main road entering the town, and six days later he rallied the Cheshire forces in the Parliamentarian defeat at Hopton Heath (Staffordshire).[16] Promoted to Brereton's adjutant-general, it can be assumed that Lothian continued to train and organise the Cheshire forces, until in mid-December 1643 he was taken prisoner after falling from his horse in a skirmish near Nantwich. In mid-July 1644 a London newsbook described him as 'Major Lothian, a gallant man lately come out of prison', confirming his release from captivity in probably early June in a prisoner exchange. Having rejoined Brereton's forces, Lothian played a leading role ordering the Cheshire Foot at Oswestry on 2 July and at Malpas on 26 August. After the former action, Sir Thomas Myddelton described him as 'Major Lothian, adjutant-general, that brave and faithful commander, to whom I cannot ascribe too much honour'.[17]

---

13 Rushworth, *Historical Collections*, Vol. 5, p. 302.
14 Markham, *Life of Robert Fairfax*, pp. 17-22.
15 HMC, *Thirteenth Report, Appendix Part I, The Manuscripts of his Grace the Duke of Portland, Volume I* (London, 1891), pp. 95-6.
16 *Cheshire's success since their pious and truly valiant colonel Sir William Brereton, baronet, came to their rescue* (London, 1643), p. 13.
17 *Copy of A Letter sent From Sir Tho. Middleton*, p. 5.

Lothian remained with the Cheshire forces throughout the First Civil War, and by 1648 held the rank of colonel. That September, during the Second Civil War, he played a leading role in the amphibious landing by Parliamentary forces on the Isle of Anglesey in north-west Wales. On 27 September the Parliamentarians led by Colonel Thomas Mytton defeated the local Royalist forces on the island in battle near Beaumaris. In his report to the speaker of the House of Commons written the following day, Mytton magnanimously acknowledged the experienced Lothian's tactical ability as an infantry commander:

> Give me leave to humbly beg one favour of your honour, that you will be pleased to acquaint the noble House that Colonel Lothian commanded the party that first entered the island and led on the foot in the battle yesterday […] and unto whom as a great means under God must be ascribed the greater part of this victory.[18]

The Royalists

Turning to the Royalist army, in command at the battle of Montgomery as regional commander-in-chief in Prince Rupert's absence was **John, Lord Byron** (*b.* 1598/9, *d.* 1652). Determined and courageous, Byron had impeccable Royalist credentials, not only for his own active military service, which extended to the Second Civil War of 1648 (and he died a Royalist exile in Paris in 1652), but also because his five brothers and an uncle were Royalist officers. However, his ability as a field commander remains debatable. While his most notable action was his single-minded governorship and lengthy and dogged defence of Chester until, tightly besieged and with no hope of relief, he surrendered the city on 3 February 1646, at both battles in which Byron held independent command, at Montgomery, and earlier at Nantwich, he was roundly defeated.

The Byrons were landed gentry from Newstead, Nottinghamshire, and in 1642 Sir John was head of the family. He had been active in county affairs, in the 1620s as MP for Nottingham, and at some point appears to have soldiered on the Continent, although the actual extent of this military experience remains obscure.[19] Hence, as Newman observed, John Byron 'illustrates the difficulty of isolating the experienced or professional soldier from the gentleman of status in domestic terms'.[20] He was a cavalry officer in the English army during the Second Bishops' War of 1640, and in December 1641 was entrusted by King Charles with the Lieutenancy, or commandantship, of the Tower of London, although in the New Year Parliament quickly forced his dismissal. In 1642 Byron's was most likely the first regiment of horse to be raised for the King's army, and it was as a competent and brave leader of cavalry that he accrued experience and repute: in leading the second line of horse of the Royalist right wing at Edgehill; in skirmishes with his regiment with the Oxford Army into spring 1643; in the West Country leading a brigade in the comprehensive Royalist victory at Roundway Down (13 July);

18 BDL, Tanner Manuscripts 57, folio 318.
19 R. Hutton, 'Byron, John, first Baron Byron (1598/9–1652)', *ODNB*, Vol. 9, p. 363.
20 Newman, *Old Service*, p. 109.

Field-Marshal-General John, Lord Byron, the acting regional commander who led the Royalist army at Montgomery. (Portrait by William Dobson, 1643. Courtesy of the University of Manchester: The Tabley House Collection)

and in commanding a larger cavalry brigade at the first battle of Newbury (Berkshire, 20 September). In reward for this service, on 24 October 1643 the King elevated Sir John to the peerage as first Baron Byron of Rochdale.

On 21 November, leading 1,300 horse and foot Lord Byron marched north from Oxford to reinforce Lord Capel and shore up the Royalist position in North Wales. Soon after arriving in theatre he was promoted field-marshal-general of Shropshire, Worcestershire, Cheshire and the six north Welsh counties. Byron was also commissioned to act in Lancashire as field-marshal and deputy to the Marquess of Newcastle, commander-in-chief of the Royalist Northern Army. It was expected that in place of Lord Capel, who arrived at Oxford on 19 December, Byron's immediate superior would be the Duke of Ormonde, the King's commander-in-chief in Ireland. In September Ormonde had settled the ceasefire in the concurrent war with the Catholic Irish Confederacy that allowed detachments of the so-called 'English-Irish' forces to be transferred to Royalist service in England and Wales.[21] In the event, however, Ormonde remained in Ireland, promoted to lord lieutenant, while Byron made Chester his headquarters. Until early January 1644 when Prince Rupert was made captain-general instead of Ormonde, Byron was left as de facto regional commander-in-chief, in charge of the Anglo-Irish reinforcements and all local forces. As has been seen, his initially successful winter campaign in Cheshire in December 1643 and into January 1644 ended in defeat at Nantwich, but he kept his command under Prince Rupert and proved a reliable deputy. Joining forces with the Prince in the northern campaign, Byron commanded the Royalist horse on the right wing at Marston Moor. Afterwards and perhaps unfairly, Byron was condemned for his faulty tactics having contributed to the defeat.[22]

Byron's major-general of horse at Montgomery was **Colonel Sir Thomas Tyldesley** (b. 1612, d. 1651). From Leigh in Lancashire, Tyldesley was one of the county's wealthiest gentlemen, and had also gained some military experience in the Continental wars.[23] He was a prominent figure in Lancashire's large minority Roman Catholic community, which gave substantial support to Charles I including provided recruits for Tyldesley's regiments of horse and foot. Arguably he was the animating force of the Lancashire Royalists. As a contemporary noted: 'There was not a man in all the county more zealous and fervent for the King's part than Colonel Thomas Tyldesley'.[24] In 1642, together with Richard, second Viscount Molyneux, another leading Lancastrian Royalist and probable fellow Catholic, Tyldesley led Lancashire forces south and fought at Edgehill. In November Tyldesley and Molyneux returned to help uphold the King's cause in Lancashire. However, after the decisive defeat of the county Royalists at Whalley on 12 April 1643, they both with their regiments progressively migrated to the Oxford Army. Tyldesley first went eastwards into Yorkshire to join the Queen and the Earl of Newcastle. In moving south with the Queen's forces towards Oxford, Sir

21 Carte, *Life of James Duke of Ormonde*, Vol. 5, pp. 510-39, *passim*; BDL, Dugdale Manuscripts 19 [first part], f. 164.
22 J. Barratt, *Cavalier Generals: King Charles and His Commanders in the English Civil War, 1642-46* (Barnsley, 2004), pp. 132-3.
23 G. Blackwood, 'Tyldesley, Sir Thomas (1612-1651)', *ODNB*, Vol. 5, pp. 764-5.
24 W. Beaumont (ed.), *A Discourse of the Warr in Lancashire* (Chetham Society, 1864), p. 19.

Thomas was knighted for his gallantry in storming the bridge at Burton-on-Trent (Staffordshire) on 2 July, and in September fought at the first battle of Newbury. In November, reunited with Molyneux Tyldesley went north again with Lord Byron. The advance of Prince Rupert's army into Lancashire in May and June 1644 allowed Tyldesley to re-recruit his regiments of horse and foot and both fought at Marston Moor, where Tyldesley probably led his horse in Byron's right wing. In August Tyldesley was with Byron and Molyneux in the defeat at Ormskirk.

Major-general of the Royalist foot was **Colonel Robert Broughton**, who, as has been seen, before the arrival of Lord Byron commanded the Royalist forces besieging Montgomery Castle. From Marchwiel, Denbighshire, Robert Broughton was a fourth son, whose eldest brother having inherited the main family estates, was inclined to seek his fortune as a soldier. In 1638 he was one of many captains returned or recalled from Continental armies to serve in the English army being formed against the Scots Covenanter regime. In 1640 during the Second Bishops' War Broughton was a captain in Sir John Merrick's Regiment of Foot,

Sir Michael Ernle (1599-1645), the Royalist area commander directing operations against Montgomery. (Portrait *circa* 1640, attributed to Adriaen Hanneman. Courtesy of Roy Precious Fine Art)

which included 200 recruits from Montgomeryshire.[25] Broughton served in Ireland from 1641 into 1643 as a captain in William Cromwell's Regiment of Foot of the army in Leinster. In February 1644 he returned to north-east Wales as Royalist colonel of what seems to have been a composite regiment of foot drawn from the army in Ireland as part of the Anglo-Irish expeditionary force. Broughton with his regiment served with Prince Rupert's regional army, and fought at Marston Moor. In Rupert's Chester-based attempted military reorganisation of later July into August Broughton was sent with reinforcements of horse and foot to Shropshire as the new military governor of Shrewsbury. He had taken up his post by 18 August.[26]

Colonel Broughton arrived at Shrewsbury accompanied by his immediate superior, **Sir Michael Ernle** (*b.* 1599, *d.* 1645). A fellow veteran of the Irish war, Ernle had only recently returned to active service after release from enemy captivity in a prisoner exchange concluded that June, having been captured at the battle of Nantwich in January.[27] Thus Ernle was not involved in Prince Rupert's northern campaign, but in August Rupert appointed him to command in Shropshire with probably the rank of major-general.

Although previous writers have stated that Ernle took part in the fighting around Montgomery, in fact he did not do so. However, as the local area

---

25 NLW, Chirk Castle Estate Records, F7442; *CSPD, 1640*, p. 467.
26 NLW, Sweeney Hall Manuscripts, folio 21.
27 In late June a Royalist correspondent reported that Ernle had returned to Chester. It seems likely that he was exchanged for the Parliamentarian Major James Lothian.

commander he played an important role in directing Royalist operations at the outset of the campaign.

Ernle, from Whetham in Wiltshire, was a highly experienced career soldier. In the late 1620s he was captain of a company of foot in one of the regiments of the English brigade, or tertia, in the service of the Dutch Republic.[28] In 1637 Ernle commanded a company in the English tertia at the siege of Breda in the southern Netherlands. A year later he was among those captains recalled to serve King Charles in the planned invasion of Scotland, and in February 1639 was promoted lieutenant-colonel of Sir Jacob Astley's Regiment of Foot. In July 1639 King Charles knighted Ernle, and in August appointed him to the important and prestigious post of governor of the border fortress of Berwick-upon-Tweed. Once hostilities against the Covenanters had ended, Ernle remained at Berwick into late 1641 overseeing the disbandment of the garrison.[29] In early 1642 he was made colonel of one of the regiments of foot newly recruited for Ireland, where he campaigned actively until later 1643. That November Ernle commanded the first and largest wave of the Anglo-Irish reinforcement landed on the Flintshire coast. His expeditionary force was the core of Lord Byron's Chester-based field army, and so Ernle was Byron's major-general of foot in the winter campaign in Cheshire. However, in Ireland Ernle had contracted consumption (tuberculosis), and so was unfit to order the infantry at the battle of Nantwich; indeed sickness may have been the reason why he was taken prisoner. Recurring illness may have prevented Ernle from assuming field command during the Montgomery campaign, but after the battle he was fit enough to become governor of Shrewsbury in place of Colonel Robert Broughton, wounded and taken prisoner of war at Montgomery. Ernle in turn was wounded and captured when Shrewsbury fell to the Parliamentarians on 22 February 1645, and he died there the following April.[30]

28 TNA, SP84/86, State Papers Foreign, Holland, folio 207.
29 *CSPD, 1638-1639*, p. 482; *CSPD, 1640*, p. 72; *CSPD, 1640-1641*, p. 276; *CSPD, 1641-1643*, p. 100.
30 Carte, *Collection of Original Letters and Papers*, p. 38; W.D. Mackay (ed.), *The History of the Rebellion and Civil Wars in England begun in the Year 1641 by Edward Earl of Clarendon* (Oxford, 1888), Vol. III, Book VIII, p. 491.

1. Montgomery Castle. View north along the ridge, from the site of the outer ward to the middle ward, and further to the substantial upstanding remains of the gatehouse and well tower of the inner ward, constructed between 1224 and 1233. Archaeological excavations took place in the 1960s, when the site was cleared of the overburden of rubble resulting from the 1649 demolition of the castle and later stone robbing. The surviving masonry was consolidated and the castle's remains are now freely accessible under the care of CADW (Welsh Historic Monuments).

2. The probable site of the battle of Montgomery, photographed from the northern end of the inner ward of Montgomery Castle. Today's agricultural landscape is probable little changed from that of the mid seventeenth century, although the prominent road heading north is an eighteenth-century turnpike.

Plate B

The opposing major-generals of horse at the battle of Montgomery: the Royalist Sir Thomas Tyldesley and the Parliamentarian Sir William Fairfax. Both men came from northern England, Tyldesley from Lancashire, Fairfax from Yorkshire, and since the outbreak of hostilities in 1642 had been militarily very active for their respective causes. Characteristically, they both fought determinedly at Montgomery. Tyldesley was taken as a prisoner of war, while Fairfax's death from wounds soon after the battle was publicised as an act of martyrdom for the Parliamentary cause.

1. Sir Thomas Tyldesley. ('Portrait of an unknown man, formerly known as Thomas Tyldesley', by an unknown artist, circa 1640s. © National Portrait Gallery, London)

2. Sir William Fairfax. (Miniature attributed to Samuel Cooper, courtesy of the Berger Collection, Denver Art Museum, Colorado)

Plate C

Royalist soldiers of the Anglo-Irish Foot. (Photo: Charles Singleton/Interpreters, L-R: Steve Stanley, Simon Frame, Spencer Houghton)

See Colour Plate Commentaries for full caption.

The cavalry mêlée at the height of the battle of Montgomery, 18 September 1644.

(Illustration by Maksim Borisov, © Helion & Company Limited)   *See Colour Plate Commentaries for full caption.*

Rank and file foot soldiers of the Royalist army. (Illustration by Maksim Borisov, © Helion & Company Limited)

See Colour Plate Commentaries for full caption.

Rank and file foot soldiers of the Parliamentary army. (Illustration by Maksim Borisov, © Helion & Company Limited)

See Colour Plate Commentaries for full caption.

VERITATE
IN
TRIVMPHO

A cornet of horse of the Parliamentary army. (Illustration by Maksim Borisov, © Helion & Company Limited)

See Colour Plate Commentaries for full caption.

6

The armies

It should not go without saying that, as in the case of most battles of this period, there are no known muster lists or other reliable contemporary records of the order of battle for either army at Montgomery. There is therefore a degree of speculation in the reconstruction of the composition and size of the opposing forces proposed here.

Organisation and tactics

Both armies were organised and armed alike, and employed similar tactics according to conventional contemporary military practice. The main fighting arms were the infantry, or foot, organised into regiments then companies; the cavalry, or horse, organised into regiments and then troops; and the artillery, or ordnance, deployed on the battlefield singly or in batteries of two or more pieces. Dragoons being mounted infantry were a useful ancillary fighting arm, combining the firepower of the foot with the mobility of the horse. Entire regiments of dragoons had been raised in the early stages of the war, but by 1644 it was more usual for companies or troops of dragoons to be attached to the regiments of horse.

The theoretical size for a regiment of foot was 1,200 men. However, even upon being raised very few regiments achieved that number, and a marching regiment mustering 500 men on campaign was strong by Civil War standards. Regiments were subdivided into companies notionally of about 100 men, but usually proportionately less according to the actual size of the regiment. Common foot soldiers were armed and equipped either as pikemen or as musketeers. Pre-war military manuals advocated an equal number of pikemen and musketeers, but during the war a ratio of one pike to two muskets was usual practice, although some units had a higher proportion of musketeers. The forces engaged in the Montgomery campaign demonstrate examples of differing practice, at a time when increasing infantry firepower was making the pike of less importance on the battlefield. While the Royalist foot at the battle included a greater number of pikemen than their Parliamentarian opponents, the foot soldiers of Sir Thomas Myddelton's Parliamentarian brigade were predominantly musket-armed; records from 1644 and into early 1645 show that the brigade was

Two views of an example of a triple-barred pott, the standard issue cavalry helmet during the English Civil Wars – commonly known as a lobster pott. A relic of the battle of Montgomery, it was found by workmen in the Lymore area in 1860 still containing the unfortunate owner's skull. This particular lobster pott is a mid-seventeenth century conversion of a fifteenth-century Italian sallet, fitted with a neck-guard and a peak with a face-guard. The cheek pieces are now missing. Note the helmet's original quilted fabric lining. (© Royal Armouries Images, courtesy of the Powysland Museum, Welshpool)

issued with about 1,100 muskets, but just 200 pikes are known to have been supplied.

The pike was a stout spear about sixteen feet in length. Used *en masse,* it had been the main offensive infantry weapon from the late fifteenth and for much of the sixteenth century, being able to outreach a horseman's lance. By the time of the Civil War the pike could still effectively keep cavalry at bay, deterring the horsemen from firing their notoriously inaccurate pistols at point-blank range. In battle, the compact blocks, or 'stands', of pikemen anchored the infantry line. They defended against cavalry and supported the musketeers, as in the example of Royalist infantry at the battle of Cheriton (Hampshire) in March 1644: 'The foot keeping their ground in a close body, not firing till within two pikes length, and then three ranks at a time, after turning up the butt end of their muskets, charging their pikes [levelling the weapon at shoulder height towards the enemy] and standing close, preserved themselves'.[1] The pike was also still a formidable offensive weapon in determined hands. As Sir John Meldrum found, for example, in October 1643 when leading what had been a successful sally by the besieged garrison of Hull against the Royalist lines: 'The violence of our soldiers was abated by 100 pikes of the enemy, who charged the van of our foot, scattered and in disorder did drive us backward again […] and enforced us all to a shameful retreat.[2]

Firing a spherical lead bullet, the smooth bore musket gave the infantry considerable firepower to an effective range of about 100 yards. The most common type was the simple and robust matchlock, fired by ignition caused by a smouldering cord (the match). Increasing numbers of the superior flintlock or snaphance, fired by ignition caused by a striking flint, were also in use. Deployed like the pikemen in ranks of files six deep, musketeers followed two forms of drill to give fire. Fire by successive ranks, where each fired in turn and then retired to reload, could be maintained in a stationary position or else, in theory, while steadily advancing upon the enemy. Firing by volleys, or 'salvees' (salvoes), three ranks at a time delivered a heavier concentration of fire. Firing by successive ranks allowed a steadier rate of fire, but the drill was complicated and so volley fire became a favoured tactic as the war progressed – used by the Royalists at Cheriton, for example, as described above. However, rapid volley fire could result in a vulnerable pause while the musketeers reloaded *en masse.* This probably encouraged the tactic of once having given two, three, or perhaps just one volley, for the musketeers, after 'turning up the butt end of their muskets' to use as clubs, quickly to attempt to engage the enemy in hand-to-hand fighting.

On the battlefield the main body of foot deployed in several 'battalia' (battalions), each having the pikes forming a central block flanked by

1   C.E.H. Chadwick Healey (ed.), *Bellum Civile: Hopton's Narrative of His Campaigns in the West (1642-1644)* (London, 1902), p. 102.
2   *A True and Exact Relation of the Great Victories Obtained by the Earl of Manchester and The Lord Fairfax Against the Earl of Newcastle's Army in the North* (London, 1643).

'sleeves' or 'wings' of musketeers. Separate blocks of musketeers could also be deployed for certain tactical tasks. Battalia were sized to retain flexibility of deployment depending on the size of the army. A contemporary sketch depicting an English army with 2,400 infantry in battle order in Ireland in 1642 shows eight battalia, each of a pike block flanked by blocks of musketeers and thus numbering 300 men, deployed in three supporting lines. It is likely in smaller Civil War battles like Montgomery that the infantry were arrayed in combined arms battalia 250-300 strong, irrespective of the size of individual regiments.[3]

Renowned and well-recruited regiments of horse could number 500 or more, subdivided into troops of 60 or so. Although on campaign the cavalry tended to retain their strength better than the infantry, units could fall substantially below strength. In Sir Thomas Myddelton's Brigade in early January 1645, for example, six troops of horse numbered just 200 officers and men, an average troop strength of just 33.[4] The horse of the Royalist and Parliamentary armies were almost entirely armed and equipped as medium cavalry, known as harquebusiers. A typical harquebusier was armed with a sword, a pair of pistols and sometimes also a flintlock carbine. They were protected by an open face helmet, steel breast and back plates or a thick leather jacket known as a buff coat, with some well-equipped horsemen wearing both. Sir William Brereton's own regiment of Cheshire Horse, for example, was accoutered in this way, and in May 1644 was to be partly re-equipped with 500 pairs of pistols, 500 hundred breast and back plates, and 500 'potts' (steel helmets).[5]

In battle the horse were usually deployed flanking the infantry on the wings of the army. Two or three troops, depending on their strength, were grouped into squadrons, or divisions, as in the case of Prince Rupert's Regiment deployed for action near Newark on 21 March 1644, 'cast out into five divisions, two troops to each division'.[6] English Civil War cavalry deployment and tactics were influenced by Dutch and by more recent Swedish practice. The former required files six deep to favour delivering pistol and carbine fire, the latter reducing the files to three deep for greater mobility and reliance on the sword. Deployment in ranks three deep became the usual preferred drill on both sides, as the tactician the Earl of Orrery observed after the Wars, describing still current practice dating from that time: 'What we generally observe and seldom or never alter whatever the

The remains of a burgonet helmet imaginatively displayed in the Old Bell Museum, Montgomery, found during archaeological excavations of the post-Civil War destruction layers at Montgomery Castle. Although a design dating from the sixteenth century, the burgonet remained in use during the English Civil War. (Courtesy of the Old Bell Museum, Montgomery. On loan to the museum and photographed with the kind permission of the Trustees of the Lymore Estate)

---

3   K. Roberts, *Pike and Shot Tactics, 1590-1660* (Oxford, 2010), pp. 57-8; S. Peachey, *The Mechanics of Infantry Combat in the First English Civil War* (Bristol, 1992), pp. 18-19, 27.
4   NLW, Chirk Castle Manuscripts 1/Biii, 93, unfoliated.
5   *Journal of the House of Commons*, Vol. 3, p. 484.
6   *His Highness Prince Rupert's Raising of the Siege at Newark Upon Trent, 21 March 1644* (Oxford, 1644).

occasion, and that is, the drawing up of our shot and pikes six deep, and our horse three deep'. However, the six deep formation continued in use as the tactical situation or ground required. At Newark in 1644, for example, Parliamentary horse were seen by the enemy to redeploy into deeper formation, 'doubling their files from three to six'.[7] Charges were delivered in close order, usually at little more than a trot or canter in order to maintain cohesion. Despite modern writers tending to imply that charging sword in hand became the preferred tactic, cavalry engagements throughout the war continued to combine swordplay with exchanges of fire. Assuming that both sides stood to fight, the one better able to time its attack gained advantage. The Parliamentarian Colonel Francis Thornhaugh, for example, reported how at the battle of Rowton Heath, fought near Chester on 24 September 1645, 'the enemy came down to us [Thornhaugh's regiment] and in a career charged; we stood and moved not till they had fired. We then clapped spurs to our horses and gave him such a charge'.[8]

The part that ordnance played in the battle of Montgomery remains obscure. The only documentary reference to artillery on either side is a passing reference to the cannon of the Parliamentarian army.[9] Round shot weighing about two pounds fired by a type of light cannon known as a Falcon or Falconet have been found in the battlefield area. Drawn by two or three horses, this is the type of mobile artillery piece of which several could have accompanied the Parliamentary army. It is most unusual that none of the contemporary Parliamentary accounts or later reports mention the capture of any Royalist ordnance, despite such prized trophies of war being usually well-publicised spoils of victory. Given the circumstances of the Royalist defeat it seems highly unlikely that they could have taken their cannon off the battlefield. Therefore, it cannot be proven that the Royalists deployed any artillery at all.

The Royalists

The Royalist army at the battle of Montgomery comprised detachments from the regional garrisons and units from Prince Rupert's field army that had fought in the northern campaign. Notwithstanding the scale of the defeat at Marston Moor, a significant part of Rupert's army had since returned to the Welsh borderland to rest and reorganise. On 10 July, eight days after the battle, around 5,000 horse and 2,000 foot of the Prince's army were reported to have rallied to him around Middleham in North Yorkshire and were expected to march for Chester. Accordingly, on 24 July the Prince with a large body of horse crossed from Lancashire into Cheshire near Runcorn via the ford on the river Mersey at Hale, while then and on following days units of Royalist foot and dragoons were ferried from Liverpool to the Cheshire side of the Mersey.[10]

7   R. Boyle, first Earl of Orrery, *A Treatise of the Art of War: Dedicated to the King's Most Excellent Majesty* (London, 1677), p. 36; *Prince Rupert's Raising of the Siege at Newark.*
8   *The Perfect Occurrences of Parliament And Chief Collections of Letters,* 3-10 Oct. 1645.
9   *CSPD, 1644-1645,* pp. 5-6.
10 Carte, *Collection of Original Letters and Papers,* p. 57; *CSPD, 1644,* p. 413.

While the post-battle reports of Sir William Brereton and Arthur Trevor both usefully name several Royalist infantry regiments present, the units forming the Royalist horse at Montgomery are less distinct.

In Arthur Trevor's relation, the action of his brother's regiment takes centre stage, and so Colonel Marcus Trevor's Regiment of Horse makes a fitting starting point in reconstructing the order of battle of the Royalist horse. The regiment had originally been Lord Capel's own, but upon arriving with Capel in Shropshire in March 1643 it had just two troops. However, successful recruitment quickly increased its size to 400 men, and the regiment became a mainstay of Capel's regional army. It remained in Shropshire after Capel's recall to Oxford in December. Forming part of the escort to a munitions convoy bound from Shrewsbury to Lord Byron's army in Cheshire, the regiment was scattered in a surprise Parliamentarian attack on the convoy when halted at Ellesmere (north Shropshire) on the night of 12/13 January 1644, and as a result was reduced to few more than a troop. Following Prince Rupert's arrival in the region the regiment was re-formed under the command of his appointee the newly promoted Colonel Marcus Trevor, who had served as a troop captain in Ireland. At its effective full strength of 400 men Trevor's Horse had fought at Marston Moor, and in early September was billeted in Denbighshire in and around the town of Ruthin.[11]

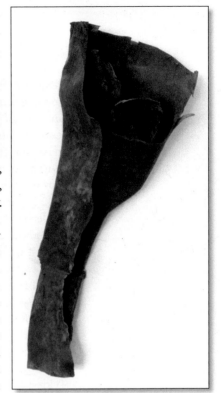

A horseman's pistol holster, made from leather, found preserved during archaeological excavations of the post-Civil War destruction layers at Montgomery Castle. A pair of pistols were the usual firearms of a Civil War cavalryman. The holsters were slung in front of the saddle. (Courtesy of the Old Bell Museum, Montgomery. On loan to the museum and photographed with the kind permission of the Trustees of the Lymore Estate)

As has been seen, Sir William Vaughan's Regiment formed part of the force from Shropshire that defeated Myddelton at Montgomery, and two Royalist accounts confirm that Vaughan was also at the battle. Since spring 1642 Vaughan had served with the army in Ireland in Leinster as a troop captain in Lord Lisle's Regiment. In early 1644 Vaughan in effect became the colonel of his own regiment when four troops of Lisle's, including Vaughan's own, numbering about 300 all ranks were shipped under his command from Dublin in early February and landed in north-east Wales near Chester. Joining Prince Rupert in Shropshire, Vaughan's Regiment fought there in March, and was with Rupert's field army at Marston Moor, where its six troops together probably numbered about 400 men.[12]

Like Vaughan, Major Thomas Dallison, the acting commanding officer of Prince Rupert's Regiment of Horse, is mentioned in Royalist correspondence as having been at the battle of Montgomery. Given his regiment's involvement in the earlier actions in Montgomeryshire, it must be assumed it fought there too. An eyewitness reported Prince Rupert's arrival at Bristol in August accompanied by 200 horsemen 'which belonged unto him'. Assuming these included the Prince's Lifeguard Troop – essentially a separate unit – along

11 Main source: HMC, *Twelfth Report, Appendix Part IX, Manuscripts of the Duke of Beaufort* (London, 1891), pp. 39-42

12 Main source: HMC, *Fourteenth Report, Appendix Part VII, Manuscripts of the Marquis of Ormonde* (London, 1895), pp. 123-4, 145-6; also, R. Symonds, *Diary of The Marches of the Royal Army During the Great Civil War kept by Richard Symonds*, (ed.) C.E. Long (The Camden Society, 1859), pp. 181, 255-6.

with one or two troops of the regiment proper, the remainder of the Prince's Horse, including the survivors of the skirmish at Newtown, probably fought at Montgomery.

In reporting his victory at Malpas, Sir William Brereton in later August identified Prince Rupert's, Vaughan's and Trevor's regiments as the most potent enemy horse in the region. He reckoned their combined strength as upwards of 1,000 men, although in fact they probably numbered somewhat less.[13] At Montgomery they were joined by the Lancashire Horse, who feature in Arthur Trevor's account: the regiments of Tyldesley and Molyneux, and, it must be assumed (although there is no direct evidence it was present) by Lord Byron's own regiment. Tyldesley and Molyneux had raised their regiments in 1642 as part of Lord Derby's Lancastrian forces. Following the decisive defeat of Derby's field army in April 1643, usually brigaded together both regiments had since served much further afield, including with the Oxford Army, and had returned north with Lord Byron in November. Formed in early summer 1642, Byron's was perhaps the most long-standing regiment of horse in the King's armies. It had served with him wherever he had been posted since.

These three regiments had fought at Marston Moor, and had fared badly in the fight at Ormskirk. They were consequently probably quite weak in numbers at the battle of Montgomery. In the wake of the defeat at Ormskirk, when the survivors were billeted with other units in the vicinity of Chester, on 22 August Will Legge wrote of them to Prince Rupert: 'But of Molyneux, Tyldesley and the Lord Byron's regiments the amount is very short, the few that kept together being here with the rest'.[14]

Together with the six regiments mentioned above, some horse from Shropshire may also have fought at Montgomery. Royalist forces in Shropshire at this time included three probably quite small regiments of horse: that of local man Sir Francis Ottley; that formed, or forming, at Ludlow under the command of a Florentine mercenary Giovanni Devillier, who had been one of the troop captains returned from Ireland under Vaughan's command in February 1644; and that commanded by another mercenary the Dutchman Colonel Johan Van Geyrish, which had been ordered to Shropshire by Prince Rupert in August 1644. All three units may have joined in the expeditionary force sent to Montgomery in early September, and so could have fought in the battle.

What is clear, however, is that the Royalist army at the battle of Montgomery did not include any Northern Horse. The detachment under Samuel Tuke's command that had joined in the attack upon Montgomery on 8 September left soon after, and by 19 September Tuke had led many of the Northern Horse to Monmouthshire. There they were billeted in an around Chepstow and Usk, while arrangements were being made to ferry them across the Severn estuary to join Prince Rupert at Bristol. Meanwhile, a second body of Northern Horse, reportedly numbering 1,300 men, including 200 or so dismounted, had continued to retreat via Worcester, passing through there

---

13 *The Success of Our Cheshire Forces, as they came Related by Sir William Brereton's own pen,* p. 4.
14 Warburton, *Prince Rupert and the Cavaliers,* Vol. 3, p. 21.

around 10 September, to Evesham and on to Broadway in the Cotswolds, making Oxford their objective.[15]

The Royalist dragoons mentioned in second-hand contemporary accounts were probably mostly from Colonel Henry Washington's Regiment. Arthur Trevor describes Washington as having played a creditable role in the battle, and a Captain Bellamy listed among Royalist prisoners taken may well have been the Captain Michael Bellamy of Washington's Dragoons, recorded in a post-Restoration list of former Royalist officers seeking a gratuity from King Charles II. During 1643 Washington's Dragoons had fought at the sieges of Bristol and Gloucester, and later joined the Banbury garrison. They spent winter 1643/4 occupying and fortifying Evesham (Worcestershire) and so came within Prince Rupert's regional command.[16] The Royalist Journal *Mercurius Aulicus* reported that Washington's Dragoons took part in the storming of Stockport in Lancashire by the Prince's army on 25 May, and they may also have fought at Marston Moor. Dragoons of Sir Vincent Corbet's Regiment, a Shropshire-based unit raised in 1642, may also have fought at Montgomery. Circumstantial evidence only, however, suggests that they may have been at the battle; in that Corbet was not present when Moreton Corbet Castle, his usual headquarters, was taken by Parliamentarians on 8 September, perhaps for the reason that he was then at Montgomery with part of his regiment.

There is more certain evidence of the order of battle of the Royalist foot at Montgomery. Sir Thomas Myddelton in his post-battle report described them as: 'the best foot in England, as the very enemies confess, being all Prince Rupert's foot, and the chosen foot out of all their garrisons'. The regiments actually named in the dispatches of Brereton and Trevor were those of Colonels Warren, Ernle, Hunckes, Broughton, Tillier, Woodhouse and Ellice.

The first five of these regiments formed part of a distinct corps within the King's armies, the so-called 'English-Irish; a misleading contemporary term for units from the English army in Ireland transferred to join the Royalists on the British mainland. Although they were portrayed in Parliamentarian propaganda as rebellious native Irish Catholics and therefore dangerous Papists, the great majority of the soldiers of the English-Irish expeditionary force were in fact English or Welsh. As one of their captains was at pains to point when negotiating with the Parliamentarian garrison of Nantwich in mid-January 1644: 'we are no Irish, but trueborn English, and real Protestants also born and bred. Pray mistake us not'.[17]

The regiments of Colonels Sir Michael Ernle and Sir Fulke Hunckes had been sent to Ireland in spring 1642 as reinforcements against the Irish uprising. On 19 November 1643 they landed at Mostyn on the Flintshire coast among the first and largest body of troops from the army in Leinster to be shipped from Dublin, numbering around 2,500 men. Colonel Henry Warren's followed, landing in Flintshire in early December. Warren's was another newly raised regiment sent to Ireland in early 1642, originally as

15 BDL, Firth Manuscripts C7, folios 157, 171, 177.
16 Carte, *A Collection of Original Letters and Papers,* p. 23.
17 Warburton, *Prince Rupert and the Cavaliers,* Vol. 2, p. 366.

the Earl of Leicester's, the then lord lieutenant of Ireland and nominally the commander-in-chief of the army there. The regiments of Colonels Robert Broughton and Henry Tillier, which, according to differing contemporary accounts, had a combined strength of 1,200 or up to 1,700 men, were shipped together with Vaughan's Horse from Dublin to north-east Wales in early-February 1644, and had joined Prince Rupert's forces in Shropshire by the end of the month. Both appear to have been composite regiments made up of drafts from other units, and probably did include several hundred native Irishmen among their ranks.[18]

The Duke of Ormonde, as lord lieutenant and commander-in-chief in Ireland their erstwhile commander, viewed the foot he had with considerable difficulty sent from Leinster in late 1643 somewhat paternally, as 'that little army […] who have already given so good proof of their constancy to the King and courage in his service'.[19] While the English-Irish regiments provided Lord Byron with a valuable corps of veteran infantry, their discipline, morale and loyalty remained uncertain as a result of the severe hardships they had experienced campaigning in the brutal war in Ireland. However, paid, re-clothed and equipped, from mid-December they proved reliable enough during Byron's winter campaign in Cheshire, so that at the close of 1643 he wrote assuring Prince Rupert that 'the world hath not braver foot nor fitter for such a general as yourself'.[20] But on 25 January 1644 at the battle of Nantwich the hard-pressed English-Irish regiments forming Byron's foot broke and were defeated, with Warren's and Ernle's regiments reportedly having performed poorly. Furthermore, many of the 1,500 or so Royalist foot taken as prisoners of war re-enlisted with the Parliamentarians. Reporting the battle to Ormonde five days later, Byron wrote requested further reinforcements, 'rather Irish than English; for the English we already have are very mutinous, and being for the most part this county-men, are so poisoned by the ill-affected people here that they grow very cold in this service'.[21]

Byron and other Royalist commanders in the region found, however, that many of the turncoats soon returned. With the regiments re-formed after Nantwich bolstered by the further reinforcements arriving from Ireland during February, the impression is that the English-Irish regiments regained their perceived esprit de corps, and as the main strength of Prince Rupert's infantry benefitted from the intense recruitment drive in force in the region during spring 1644. While Hunckes's remained to garrison Shrewsbury, Warren's, Ernle's, Broughton's and Tillier's regiments fought in the northern campaign and at Marston Moor. Like other units of Rupert's army defeated and scattered, but not wholly broken at the battle, the English-Irish regiments were re-formed during Prince Rupert's reorganisation in late July and August, although because of casualties, sickness, straggling and desertion they must have been heavily re-recruited. However, if, as seems likely, a company or

---

18 *Mercurius Aulicus*, 25 Nov. 1643; BDL, Firth Manuscripts C6, folios 11, 74; M. Stoyle, *Soldiers And Strangers: An Ethnic History of the English Civil War* (New Haven and London, 2005), p. 209.

19 Carte, *A Collection of Letters, Written by the Kings Charles I and II*, p. 232.

20 William Salt Library, Prince Rupert's Papers, SMS 485.

21 Carte, *Collection of Original Letters and Papers*, p. 39.

two of each regiment had remained in the regional garrisons during the northern campaign, these would have provided a cadre around which the regiments could rally. Such an arrangement may have allowed Sir Michael Ernle's regiment in particular to be re-formed at Chester or Shrewsbury. When Sir Marmaduke Langdale had withdrawn from southern Cumbria and northern Lancashire a local commander had ordered most of Ernle's men to remain in the Furness peninsula, from where the Royalist outpost at Carlisle was considered to offer their only hope of a safe retreat![22] Evidence of the recruitment and re-equipping of Tillier's regiment, which seems to have suffered particularly heavy losses at Marston Moor, is provided by the new uniforms made in green, the regimental colour, stored at the Red Castle at Welshpool.[23] However, it seems unlikely that any of the English-Irish regiments could have numbered many more than 300 men by the time of the Montgomery campaign.

Of the two other Royalist infantry regiments named as having fought at Montgomery, Sir Michael Woodhouse's regiment had been raised during spring 1643 and recruited from the counties of Lord Capel's command as the Prince of Wales's Lifeguard of Foot. Woodhouse was another English veteran of the war in Ireland, who returned to serve the King in early 1643 and became Capel's sergeant-major-general of foot. In summer 1643 the Lifeguard under Woodhouse's command was detached to the Oxford Army, and in September numbering about 700 men fought at the first battle of Newbury.[24] In early October the regiment rejoined Capel's army in Shropshire, where if remained thereafter as the mainstay of Woodhouse's garrison at Ludlow. While it saw occasional action in the region during 1644, Woodhouse's Foot – the Lifeguard appellation seems to have been dropped – did not take part in Rupert's northern campaign and so was one of the stronger units of Royalist foot at Montgomery.

Colonel Robert Ellice, a professional soldier who had served in the Swedish army during the Thirty Years' War, seems to have raised a regiment of foot in his native Denbighshire over winter 1642/3. Numbering about 600 men, the regiment was broken in Brereton's victory at Middlewich in March 1643 when Ellice was taken prisoner. Released from captivity that September, Ellice set about re-forming his regiment, and in November received a new commission from Charles I to raise 1,200 men; this may have been as a result of the Parliamentarian invasion of north-east Wales, when Ellice's men had again fared badly. Ellice's Foot joined Prince Rupert's forces in Shropshire in spring 1644, and during the Prince's advance into Lancashire fought at the storming of Bolton on 28 May. The regiment had remained in Lancashire, perhaps occupying Bolton, but later joined the Royalist retreat to Chester and north-east Wales. By early September Ellice had billeted his regiment, reportedly numbering only about 200 men, in the castle and town of Denbigh.[25]

22 BDL, Firth Manuscripts C7, folio 149.

23 Symonds, *Diary*, p. 255; *The True Informer*, 10-17 Aug. 1644.

24 W.A. Day (ed.), *The Pythouse Papers: Correspondence Concerning The Civil War, the Popish Plot and a Contested Election in 1680* (London, 1879), p. 16.

25 R. Williams (ed.), 'An Account of the Civil War in North Wales, Transcribed from the MS Notebook of William Maurice, esq., Preserved in the Wynnstay Library', *Archaeologica*

Although the evidence for their involvement is more circumstantial, several other regiments of Royalist infantry must also be assumed to have fought at Montgomery.

Prince Rupert's Regiment of Foot, under the command of Lieutenant-colonel John Russell, had marched from Bristol to join the Prince in Shropshire in early March 1644. About 600 strong it was one of the larger infantry regiments in the Prince's field army, and during the northern campaign fought at Bolton, where it suffered significant casualties, and at Marston Moor. The regiment did not follow Prince Rupert to Bristol in later August, and in early October was based at Chester under Byron's command, who reported to the Prince that it was 'much lessened' – partly due to desertion, but probably also as a result of losses sustained at Montgomery.[26]

Lord Byron appears to have formed his own regiment of foot at Chester in March 1644, around a nucleus of five under-strength companies of foot, including native Irish as well as English soldiers, sent as reinforcements from Dublin in early March. A month later, Byron reckoned that his own regiment, and that of his brother Colonel Robert Byron (another of the English-Irish regiments landed in November 1643) and the Lancashire foot of Sir Thomas Tyldesley together numbered about 1,000 rank and file. Byron's Foot fought in the northern campaign and at Marston Moor, and later were the mainstay of Byron's Chester garrison. That at least a detachment of the regiment fought at Montgomery is suggested by the fact that Captain Roger Manley, one of its company commanders, and another claimant of the post-Restoration royal gratuity, after the battle had taken refuge at the Red Castle near Welshpool.[27]

Given that Colonel Richard Herbert was in Shropshire in early September 1644, and that he had a vested interest in the outcome of events at Montgomery, it seems likely that his regiment also fought in the battle. As has been seen, Herbert began to recruit a regiment of foot in and around Montgomeryshire and Shropshire in autumn 1642, and he took it to join the Oxford Army in January 1643.[28] Herbert's Foot campaigned with the Oxford Army and under Prince Rupert until the autumn. In late September it marched from Oxford in company with Sir Michael Woodhouse's Regiment to return to Shropshire, where Herbert had been appointed as governor of Ludlow. His regiment remained in the central Marches in early 1644, when it was probably based at Montgomery (providing, as had been seen, justification for Lord Herbert to reject Prince Rupert's proposal of establishing a permanent garrison there), and in April formed part of Sir Michael Woodhouse's force besieging Brampton Bryan castle in northern Herefordshire.[29] It must be assumed that Herbert took his men to Aberystwyth after being appointed governor there in April, but the actual movements of the regiment remain obscure. The listing of one Major Williams among the captured Royalists may indicate

Cambrensis (1846), pp. 34-5; P. Young, *Marston Moor 1644 – The Campaign and the Battle* (Moreton-in Marsh, 1997), pp. 195-6; *The Perfect Occurrences of Parliament And Chief Collections of Letters*, 6-13 Sept. 1644.

26 Young, *Marston Moor*, pp. 13, 195; BDL, Firth Manuscripts C7, folio 196.

27 Carte, *A Collection of Letters, Written by the Kings Charles I and II*, p. 256; BDL, Firth Manuscripts C7, folio 24; BL, Additional Manuscripts 18981, folio 281.

28 *Mercurius Aulicus*, 14 Jan. 1643.

29 BL, Additional Manuscripts 18981, folios 67, 152.

that Herbert's Foot did fight at Montgomery. He may well have been Major Edward Williams, the regiment's deputy commander who had led it in the assault on Bristol in July 1643.[30]

Sir Thomas Tyldesley's Regiment of Foot is another infantry unit that may have been at Montgomery. Originally formed in November 1642 by Tyldesley in Lancashire, since the Royalist defeat there in spring 1643 the regiment had fought as part of the Oxford Army, at the storming of Bristol, at the siege of Gloucester and at the first battle of Newbury. Together with Tyldesley's own, Lord Byron's and Lord Molyneux's regiments of horse, Tyldesley's Foot had formed a large proportion of the 1,200 or so horse and foot – 'most from Lancashire' – that Byron led to the northern Marches in November 1643. Prince Rupert's campaign in Lancashire from May into June 1644 gave Tyldesley the opportunity to recruit, and probably for that reason Barratt has supposed his was the largest of Prince Rupert's infantry regiments at Marston Moor, numbering 1,000 men. In August Tyldesley's Foot were attached to Molyneux's brigade of horse with Lord Byron covering Lancashire, but probably suffered heavy losses in the defeat at Ormskirk. The remainder may well have fought at Montgomery, although there were probably few of them and Tyldesley himself fought with his cavalry as major-general of the Royalist horse.[31]

A final body of Royalist foot at Montgomery may have been drawn from the region's trained bands. The trained bands were the standing body and best equipped and practised of the militia of early Stuart England and Wales. Lord Byron instructed the commissioners of array in Montgomeryshire and neighbouring counties to make ready the trained bands and await his further orders, and by the time of his arrival at Montgomery on 17 September some trained bands companies may have made their way there.[32] The trained bands of Montgomeryshire and Shropshire, for example, had pre-war strengths of 300 and 600 rank and file respectively. The Shropshire captains and their companies went over to the Royalists in 1642, and it can be inferred that the Montgomeryshire trained bands did the same. More certainly, the town records from Bridgnorth for 1644 mention a gratuity paid to several townsmen who as trained band soldiers had been at the siege of Montgomery Castle – thus proving that a detachment of the Shropshire trained bands at least was present.[33]

Contemporary estimates of the size of the Royalist army at the battle of Montgomery of course vary considerably. On the Parliamentarian side, in their post-battle dispatches Sir Thomas Myddelton stated that the enemy had numbered 5,000, while Sir William Brereton reckoned the Royalists were 'no less than 4,000'. The Parliamentarian chronicler John Rushworth agreed that there were about 4,000 Royalists. Arthur Trevor provides the only known Royalist estimation, reiterating his brother's first-hand account that Byron's

30 Warburton, *Prince Rupert and the Cavaliers*, Vol. 2, p. 237.
31 J.M. Gratton, *The Parliamentarian and Royalist War Effort in Lancashire 1642-1651* (Manchester, 2010), p. 315; Phillips, *Civil War in Wales and the Marches*, Vol. 2, p. 105; J. Barratt, *The Battle of York: Marston Moor 1644* (Stroud, 2002), pp. 151, 162.
32 Parry, *Royal Visits and Progresses to Wales*, p. 386.
33 Shropshire Archives, Bridgnorth Corporation Collection, BB/D/1/2/1/54: chamberlains' account roll for year 1644.

army had 3,500 men. However, Marcus Trevor with his regiment would have marched with Byron's reinforcements, and so he may not have fully known the number of Royalists already engaged besieging Montgomery Castle. The contemporary Welsh diarist William Maurice recorded that Byron marched to Montgomery with 3,000 men, a figure according with Marcus Trevor's estimate had he mainly taken account of Byron's division from Chester and north-east Wales.

Simply taking the mean average of these five estimates puts the Royalists at 3,900 men. However, this seems a little low when the units already at Montgomery upon Byron's arrival on 17 September are taken into account. Therefore, it seems more likely that the combined Royalist army numbered about 4,400 men, comprising two-thirds foot and one third horse.

The Parliamentarians

Like the Royalists, the Parliamentarian army included detachments from regional county forces and garrison regiments, drawn from four distinct commands: Sir Thomas Myddelton's Brigade; the Earl of Denbigh's Army of the West Midlands Association; Sir William Brereton's Cheshire forces; and the Lancashire forces, temporarily under Sir John Meldrum's leadership. At this time both of the latter county forces can be considered as small regional armies in their own right.

Coordinated operations between neighbouring county forces, or between adjoining associations of counties grouped into regional commands, for both sides during the First Civil War were often beset with difficulties of command and coordination. The success of the combined Parliamentarian army at Montgomery, independent of the attempted strategic directions of the Committee of Both Kingdoms in London, was therefore notable. In hopeful expectation that Meldrum could keep the army together and mount further operations, on 27 September the Committee belatedly commended to him their wish that 'this experience of the advantage of cooperation and conjunction of forces will be a means both to strengthen your union […] and improve all opportunities against the enemy'.[34] Notwithstanding the fact that the army had by then dispersed, and by the time Meldrum received the Committee's dispatch he was on his way to return to the siege at Liverpool, for the short time it was in being the Parliamentarian army that fought at Montgomery demonstrated that successful collaborative action at a regional level was achievable.

The main strength of the Parliamentarian infantry was the Cheshire Foot of Sir William Brereton's army. By summer 1644 there were six regiments of Cheshire Foot – Sir William's own, and those of Colonels George Booth, Henry Brooke, Robert Duckenfield, John Leigh and Henry Mainwaring. Like Brereton, the other colonels were landowning Cheshire gentry, and so their regiments tended to be officered and recruited from their landed estates within the different county hundreds forming the administrative districts of Cheshire. Thus Booth's regiment came mostly from the town and southerly hundred of Nantwich; Brooke's from northerly Bucklow hundred;

---

34 *CSPD, 1644*, pp. 537-8.

Duckenfield's from easterly Macclesfield hundred and the Stockport area; Leigh's from Bucklow and the central hundreds of Eddisbury and Northwich; and Mainwaring's mainly from Northwich. In a muster list of the Cheshire Forces dated 30 April 1645, Brereton's own regiment, by far the largest, and with 1,520 men in effect a double regiment, is described as being ready 'upon instant duty'; an indication that it was more widely recruited and less locally based than the other regiments, which probably included a significant proportion of militiamen. In April 1645 these six regiments together numbered more than 4,100 men, including three companies of attached dragoons (Brereton's regiment of dragoons by then having been disbanded).[35] Assuming that the strength of the Cheshire Foot in early autumn 1644 was not much less, and that was probably the case, then it can be seen how Brereton was able not only to provide most of the infantry for the Montgomery campaign, but had sufficient reserves to hold the garrisons recently established facing Chester together with his other Cheshire bases, while also posting three companies to Shropshire.

By the time of the battle of Montgomery, the Cheshire Foot were a well experienced, if not veteran, body of infantry by English Civil War standards, a status reflected by their performance in the battle. Their steadiness, and musketry fire in particular, had been remarked upon in recent engagements in Shropshire, Lancashire and Cheshire. After the Parliamentarian victory outside Oswestry on 2 July, in his dispatch reporting the action to Parliament Sir Thomas Myddelton described how:

> I had to my aid three regiments of foot, viz Colonel George Booth's Regiment, a
> gallant regiment led by himself on foot, to the face of the enemy; another [led] by
> Colonel Mainwaring, and the third by Colonel Croxton,[36] all of them stout and
> gallant commanders, and the rest of the officers and soldiers full of courage and
> resolution.

In August, Leigh's regiment had performed well at Tarvin, the firepower of Booth's regiment had first unsettled the Royalists at Ormskirk, while the seven companies from Brook's, Duckenfield's and Brereton's regiments engaged at Malpas, according to Sir William, 'had performed very good execution', despite having been outflanked and partly encircled by the Royalist horse at one point during the action.

The remaining Parliamentarian infantry in Meldrum's relief force were the 'other companies from Stafford' described by Thomas Malbon and mentioned in other reports. These were companies of the Staffordshire regiment of Colonel Simon Rugeley, ostensibly part of the Earl of Denbigh's West Midland Association Army, although by this time the Earl had returned to London and was no longer exercising direct command. Rugeley was one

35 R.N. Dore (ed.), *The Letter Books of Sir William Brereton, Volume I, January 31st–May 29th 1645* (Gloucester, 1984), pp. 324-32.

36 Myddelton seems to have misreported Thomas Croxton's rank; he was major of Brereton's regiment in 1645, but was probably acting lieutenant-colonel when leading part of the regiment at Oswestry. Extract from *A Copy of A Letter sent From Sir Tho. Middleton […].*

of Staffordshire's leading Parliamentarians, and had also raised a regiment of horse. He led his foot soldiers in person at Montgomery.[37]

Meldrum does not seem to have led any of the Lancashire Foot to Montgomery, who instead remained there maintaining the siege of Liverpool and blockading a couple of other isolated Royalist garrisons. Similarly, there appears no evidence that any units of the Shropshire forces, at this time still nominally under Colonel Mytton's overall command, or that Mytton himself fought at Montgomery. The departure of Myddelton's Brigade into Montgomeryshire had dangerously weakened the strength of the garrisons at Oswestry and Wem, causing the Shropshire Parliamentarians to request reinforcements from Brereton. Although having captured Moreton Corbet Castle, the Shropshire Parliamentarians had insufficient strength to also commit forces to Meldrum's relief army.

The detachments of Yorkshire Horse from Lord Fairfax's army of the Northern Association under Sir William Fairfax's command formed the main body of cavalry in Meldrum's army. To date, Lord Fairfax's army has not been researched in any detail, so the composition of Sir William's division posted to Lancashire remains unknown. It included his own regiment, together with detachments from any of the nine (according to Barratt) or eight (according to Tincey) regiments of Northern Association Horse with the allied army at Marston Moor.[38] Given the limited role that cavalry could perform against the remaining besieged or beleaguered Royalist garrisons in Lancashire, it is likely that most of Fairfax's 1,000 or so horsemen joined Meldrum's army for the relief of Montgomery Castle. Sir William Brereton's own regiment was the second largest contingent of horse, being the sole cavalry regiment of the Cheshire forces. In April 1645 the regiment numbered 790 men in 13 troops, making it a very large regiment by Civil War standards.[39] Before Montgomery troops of Brereton's Horse had fought successfully in the actions during August at Tarvin and at Malpas. The Lancastrian forces probably contributed some troops of horse to Meldrum's army. There was no amalgamated county regiment until 1645, and so the Lancashire Horse at this time comprised several independent troops attached to the infantry regiments; such as the troop of Colonel Ralph Ashton, who had also raised and commanded one of the larger regiments of Lancashire Foot.[40] The remaining horsemen in the Parliamentarian army were those of Sir Thomas Myddelton's Brigade who had retreated with him to Oswestry. Given their losses sustained in escaping from Montgomery, and allowing for those who may have retreated to Montgomery Castle during the Royalist attack, Myddelton's horse and dragoons at the battle probably numbered about 200.

37 Malbon, 'Memorials of the Civil War', p. 147; *The Kingdomes Weekly Intelligencer*, 24 Sept.-1 Oct. 1644.

38 Barratt, in *Battle for York*, p. 166 lists Sir William Fairfax's, Lord Fairfax's and Sir Thomas Fairfax's regiments, together with those of Sir William Constable, Sir Thomas Norcliffe and Colonels John Lambert, Charles Fairfax, Hugh Bethell and Christopher Copley. Tincey, in *Marston Moor 1644: The beginning of the End* (London, 2003), p. 91, differs in listing eight regiments of Northern Association Horse: the regiments of Lord Fairfax, Sir Thomas and Charles Fairfax (but not Sir William's), Norcliffe, Lambert and Bethel, Colonel Francis Boynton, and Lionel, rather than Christopher, Copley.

39 Dore, *Letter Books of Sir William Brereton, Volume 1*, p. 385.

40 Gratton, *Parliamentarian and Royalist War Effort in Lancashire*, pp. 280-300.

In their post battle dispatches Meldrum, Brereton and Myddelton numbered the Parliamentarian army at about 3,000 men, in approximately equal numbers of mounted and foot. This seems a low estimation, perhaps resulting from their reckonings not having included officer ranks. Rushworth put the size of Meldrum's army at '3,000 and upwards', while the London newsbook the *Scottish Dove*, published on 27 September 1644, and perhaps drawing on additional information, reported that the army had numbered 'less than 4,000'.

According to Thomas Malbon, Meldrum's army had 32 troops of horse, an estimate that probably did not include Myddelton's mounted contingent. If the average strength of these 32 troops was 47 (all ranks) – a reasonable mean for Civil War horse; the 13 troops of Brereton's regiment in April 1645, for example, averaged 60 men – then Meldrum had about 1,700 cavalry, Myddelton's horsemen included. It seems more likely, then, that the Parliamentarian army at the battle of Montgomery was about 3,400 strong, approximately equally divided between horse and foot. In addition, most of Myddelton's original force of 500 infantrymen occupied the castle, a large garrison that would influence the outcome of the battle.

Conclusions

Both armies were similarly ad-hoc formations, although formed from fewer and larger units the Parliamentarian army was more cohesive. The Royalist army consisted mostly of what could be termed veteran regiments from Prince Rupert's Welsh borderlands army. These still had many experienced soldiers, but as a result of attrition in the northern campaign and elsewhere since also included many inexperienced recruits. Therefore the morale and fighting ability of these units was suspect. Many of the Royalist cavalry in particular seem to have been campaign weary and somewhat demoralised. One wonders, too, of the effect on Royalist morale of the untimely hasty departure of Prince Rupert, hitherto their charismatic commander-in-chief. The soldiers of the Parliamentarian army, on the other hand, would have been heartened by the recent series of victories gained over the enemy. The regiments of Sir William Brereton's Cheshire army in particular by this stage of the war were reliable units with high morale. From what we can tell, on the day of the battle the mettle of Meldrum's army, man for man, was greater than that of Byron's.

Orders of Battle

The orders of battle reconstructed here are necessarily somewhat conjectural. Numbers are speculative, but take into account the recent service and campaign history of each unit. It should be borne in mind that not all regiments listed were entirely engaged at Montgomery, with detachments remaining on garrison duty elsewhere. Sir Michael Woodhouse's Regiment, for example, was probably one of the largest Royalist units, but it seems likely that part it would have remained in garrison at Ludlow in Shropshire.

Royalist Order of Battle
Officer commanding: Field-marshal-general John, Lord Byron

The Horse: Major-general Colonel Sir Thomas Tyldesley

Prince Rupert's Regiment	200 all ranks
Sir William Vaughan's Regiment	300 all ranks
Colonel Marcus Trevor's Regiment	300 all ranks
Lord Byron's Regiment	150 all ranks
Sir Thomas Tyldesley's Regiment	150 all ranks
Lord Molyneux's Regiment	150 all ranks
Shropshire Horse, detachments?	150 all ranks

Dragoons

Colonel William Washington's Regiment	100 all ranks
Colonel Sir Vincent Corbet's Regiment?	50 all ranks

The Foot: Major-general Colonel Robert Broughton

Colonel Henry Warren's Regiment	250 all ranks
Sir Michael Ernle's Regiment	200 all ranks
Sir Fulke Hunckes's Regiment	300 all ranks
Colonel Robert Broughton's Regiment	250 all ranks
Colonel Henry Tillier's Regiment	300 all ranks
Sir Michael Woodhouse's Regiment	400 all ranks
Colonel Robert Ellice's Regiment	200 all ranks
Price Rupert's Regiment	200 all ranks
Lord Byron's Regiment	200 all ranks
Colonel Richard Herbert's Regiment	200 all ranks
Sir Thomas Tyldesley's Regiment	100 all ranks
Trained Band Companies	250 all ranks

Total of army: about 4,400

Parliamentarian Order of Battle
Officer commanding: Sir John Meldrum

Fellow commanding officers: Sir Thomas Myddelton and Sir William Brereton

The Horse: Major-general Colonel William Fairfax

The Yorkshire Horse, detachments	900 all ranks
Sir William Brereton's Regiment	400 all ranks
The Lancashire Horse, detachments	200 all ranks
Sir Thomas Myddelton's horse and dragoons	200 all ranks

The Foot: Major-general Major James Lothian

The Cheshire Foot,	1,400 all ranks
comprising detachments from six regiments	
The Staffordshire Foot,	300 all ranks
Colonel Simon Rugeley's Regiment	

Garrison of Montgomery Castle:

The foot of Sir Thomas Myddelton's Brigade	450-500 all ranks

Total of army: about 3,900

7

In search of the battlefield

The site of the battle of Montgomery has still to be exactly and securely located. Visitors to the area today will not find a battlefield monument, or a memorial to a notable casualty of the action. Although the fighting on 18 September 1644 resulted in several hundred deaths, and the critically wounded would have died in and around Montgomery for some time afterwards, there are no known burials of the fallen (the records of the town's sole parish church do not survive from this time), or recorded discoveries of burial pits on the town's wider hinterland where the battlefield lies.[1]

The larger-scale mapping of Montgomeryshire by the Ordnance Survey, undertaken and published between 1885 and 1896, does, however, confidently mark the battlefield. It was situated by the late Victorian surveyors on the five inches to one-mile scale map in fields less than a mile north-east of the centre of Montgomery, near the County Boundary bridge – so called because it stands within yards of the English border with Shropshire. The modern bridge here carries over a stream-carved ravine the B4386, the easterly road into Montgomery originally laid as a turnpike road around 1768.

The Ordnance Survey sited the battlefield in association with the County Boundary bridge because an unnamed bridge is one of the few topographical features mentioned in contemporary records of the battle. Meldrum's first-hand account and Rushworth's later history both refer to an unnamed bridge that the Parliamentarian army secured on its arrival in the Montgomery area on 17 September. This bridge, according to Meldrum, became a tactical objective for the Royalists during the battle, which had they taken it would have endangered a Parliamentarian retreat.

The only other readily identifiable man-made and natural features of the wider battlefield landscape mentioned in contemporary accounts are the castle and town of Montgomery (although the town itself does not seem to

---

1   This chapter draws on the Clwyd-Powys Archaeological Trust's *Historic Landscape Characterisation: The Vale of Montgomery* as the main secondary topographical and historical source: Available (summer 2015): www.cpat.org.uk/projects. The author is grateful to Carrie White, and, in particular, to John Davies, local historians of Montgomery and Montgomeryshire, who responded generously to my enquiries regarding the early routeways of Montgomeryshire. Estate maps from the Powis Castle Estate Records at the NLW, dated 1820 (shelf mark M235 037/2) and 1761 (shelf mark M232 037/2), proved useful in determining the older routes around Montgomery.

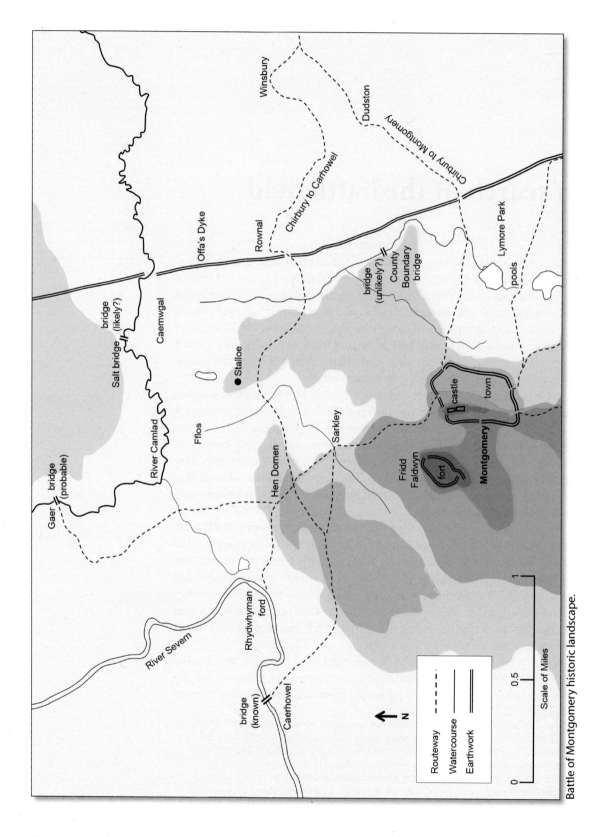

Battle of Montgomery historic landscape.

have been fought over), and the 'mountain above the castle' mentioned by Myddelton (and reiterated by Rushworth). The Royalist army withdrew to this high ground upon the arrival of Meldrum's army and spent the night before the battle there. This so-called mountainous area is the massif of undulating hill country to the west and south-west of Montgomery, which further westward descends to the floodplain of the river Severn. The town lies on the low eastern slopes below Montgomery Castle, standing on the high ground proper. The castle is in turn overlooked by the higher summit of Fridd Faldwyn, the 'mountain' itself, crowned by the prehistoric hill fort. The Royalists had beleaguered the castle from this high ground, and it would have provided a suitably expansive camping ground for Byron's army on the eve of the battle.

Myddelton also mentions some advantageous ground near Montgomery occupied by Meldrum's army on 17 September, a position that the Royalists had abandoned on the Parliamentarian approach. The Parliamentarians camped here overnight, positioned not far from the town; Rushworth described how 'on the 17th of September, they came up to Montgomery, and lay that night at a small distance in the field'.

Identifying the site of the bridge would help locate the battlefield. However, very little is known about the bridges and the roads (which in fact were mostly un-metalled trackways, poorly constructed and maintained) in the vicinity of Montgomery and across Montgomeryshire prior to the modernising turnpike acts of the later eighteenth and early nineteenth century, which transformed the road network. The roads around Montgomery were altered and improved at this time, so that the modern main roads follow the course of the turnpikes.

The two rivers in the area are the Severn, at its nearest point about a mile and a half north-west of Montgomery, and the Camlad, a less significant watercourse crossing the vale of Montgomery east to west due north of the town.

The only crossing of a watercourse in the Montgomery area that confidently can be assumed to have been bridged at the time of the Civil War was that over the river Severn at Caerhowel, nearly two miles north-west of Montgomery and sited 300 yards downstream from the site of the modern (post turnpike) bridges. A succession of timber bridges had stood at Caerhowel since the mid-thirteenth century, on the line of the main medieval east-west routeway crossing the vale of Montgomery into the upper Severn valley. The late medieval bridge supplanted the ancient crossing of the Severn at the ford at Rhydwhyman, 500 yards further downstream. The bridge at Caerhowel historically was variously known as the Montgomery bridge, the Severn bridge and the New bridge, and is recorded in Montgomeryshire's early eighteenth century quarter session records – the earliest known administrative records mentioning the county's public bridges.[2]

The session records for 1713 also mention the Gaer bridge crossing the Camlad in Forden parish two miles north-north-west of Montgomery. There was probably a bridge here at the time of the Civil War, carrying an older

---

2   Powys Archives, M/QS/SO/1, Montgomeryshire Quarter Sessions Order Book, 1707-1737.

north-south route towards Montgomery, but it lies too far to the north of the likely battlefield area, and so can be discounted.

The sites of two other modern crossings in the Montgomery area may also have been bridged in the seventeenth century, but the evidence is uncertain.

As has been seen, the Victorian Ordnance Survey assumed that the County Boundary bridge was the bridge associated with the battle. However, this had not been a crossing point for either of the two known main late medieval and early modern pre-turnpike roads running east to west across the vale of Montgomery: that to the north of the town, heading from Chirbury in the direction of the Severn crossing at Caerhowel/Rhydwhyman, and further south, the way from Chirbury to Montgomery. While the modern B4386 road from Chirbury, the next largest settlement on the way to Shrewsbury, and pre-dating Montgomery, follows the direct line of the eighteenth century turnpike over the County Boundary bridge towards Montgomery, the now lost or indistinct course of the two earlier routes was more circuitous, connecting settlements that today have become farms or shrunken hamlets. An estate map shows that the meandering northerly Chirbury to Caerhowel routeway was still in use in 1761. Similarly, an estate map from 1785 depicts the old Chirbury to Montgomery road as still approaching the town towards the site of the easterly late medieval town gate.[3] The same map suggests that the new turnpike had cut across pre-existing field boundaries. Coupled with the straightness of the new road, this does not suggest that the turnpike overlaid an earlier main route into Montgomery. John Ogilby's *Britannia*, an atlas of the kingdom's main roads published in 1675, gives no clear indication as to whether the Shrewsbury and Bridgnorth road mentioned, meaning the same main road out of Shropshire approaching Montgomery from the east, was the medieval Chirbury to Montgomery road, or another way taking the same direct route as the later turnpike.[4] Furthermore, both the Chirbury to Caerhowel and the Chirbury to Montgomery routes remained in use after the opening of the Chirbury to Montgomery turnpike. As a result, both were ordered to be closed and disused to prevent their use by travellers seeking to avoid paying the turnpike toll. It seems unlikely, therefore, that a bridge stood on the site of the modern County Boundary bridge at the time of the battle, or if one did, that it was not particularly important to local communication.

Previous researchers of the battle have, however, tended to assume that the bridge stood on the site of the modern Salt bridge, crossing the river Camlad one and a half miles or so due north of Montgomery. There is some anecdotal evidence that remains of an earlier timber bridge were found here, while the suggested derivation of Salt from the Welsh 'Is Allt', as meaning under the ascent of a steep hill, indicates the locations antiquity and certainly suits its topographical location, being immediately overlooked by an escarpment to the north. It is tempting to identify this as the 'Pont-y-Cymbe' – in Welsh, the bridge in a valley or hollow – mentioned in Parry's transcription of

---

3   The author is grateful to Ann and John Welton, the curators of the Old Bell Museum in Montgomery, for bringing the museum's copy of this map to my attention.

4   J. Ogilby, *Britannia, or an Illustration of the Kingdom of England and Dominion of Wales by a Geographical and Historical Description of the Principal Roads thereof* (London, 1675).

the Mostyn manuscript as the bridge where on 8 September the Royalists caught up with Myddelton's horsemen fleeing from Montgomery and almost captured the general himself. Cymbe, or correctly in Welsh, Cwm may be linked phonetically to Caemwgal, the name given to the immediate area and nearby farm, from the Welsh suggesting a low lying area where smoke or mist could hang.[5] However, such tentative connections should not be taken too far. The straight modern road from Montgomery over the Salt bridge follows the turnpike built around 1756.[6] The 'Welshpool road' indicated heading in a northerly direction from the town on the 1761 estate map is therefore the new turnpike. Hence, it remains uncertain whether there was an earlier route heading this way to the Salt bridge site. Had there been, it would have passed the farm at Stalloe, half a mile due south of Salt bridge, where a substantial farm stood at the time of the battle on a site occupied since the Middle Ages. An otherwise insignificant bridge, locally useful to the farm at Stalloe and carrying a trackway north from Montgomery across the Camlad, may therefore have stood at the Salt bridge site in 1644.

Reconstructing the route taken by the opposing armies marching to Montgomery may provide a clearer indication of the location of the bridge and the battlefield. Both the Mostyn manuscript and the contemporary Welsh diarist William Maurice recorded that Lord Byron's army from Chester and the north-east Wales garrisons marched from Denbighshire into Montgomeryshire following the northerly stretch of the Chester to Bristol road, traversing the hill country to the west of the Severn valley via the villages of Llansillin and Llanfyllin. The road lay near the Royalist garrison at Chirk Castle, which was probably the initial rendezvous and mustering point for Byron's forces. The Mostyn manuscript goes on to mention that Byron's march continued south to the village of Berriew, some five miles north-west of Montgomery across the Severn valley. Crossing there the river Rhiw, a minor tributary of the Severn, a little to the south of Berriew the army camped in the parkland around Vaynor Hall on 16 September. Having crossed the Severn by the Caerhowel bridge, Byron's reinforcements arrived in the vicinity of Montgomery the next day.

Unfortunately, there are no similar accounts of the route taken by Meldrum's army. On 15 September munitions for 'the relief of Montgomery', comprising six barrels of gunpowder, six hundredweight of match and one thousand weight of musket ball, were issued from Myddelton's magazine at Oswestry.[7] This suggests that the army was then in the area, when these munitions would have been added to the supply train. The only other clue as to the direction of the army's march to Montgomery is a tantalising reference in the Mostyn manuscript to Wattlesborough Heath, then an expansive area of uncultivated common land 11 miles west of Shrewsbury and about the same distance north-east of Montgomery. Perhaps gathered here on 16 September,

---

5   CPAT, *Historic Landscape Characterisation*; Anon., 'Place Names In and Around Montgomery', *Collections Historical and Archaeological relating to Montgomeryshire and its Borders* (1891), pp. 224-32.

6   A. Howell, 'The Roads, Bridges, Canals and Railways of Montgomeryshire', *Collections Historical and Archaeological relating to Montgomeryshire and its Borders* (1875), pp. 313-334.

7   NLW, Chirk Castle Manuscripts 1/Biii, 93.

View southward towards Montgomery across the probable battlefield area. The furthest ridge, climbed by the road in the far distance, may be where the Royalist army deployed.

the Parliamentarian army would have had a choice of routeways out of Shropshire: either to march south-west down the Rea valley, or to take a longer but near parallel route, following the Long Mountain ridgeway from Westbury arriving at Forden north of Montgomery. Both routes followed the course of Roman roads that had remained in use as later byways. Either way would have brought the Parliamentarians within reach of patrols from Royalist occupied Caus Castle near Westbury; but as with the foray by horse from the Red Castle brushed aside by Myddelton's Brigade passing Welshpool on 4 September, any such enemy intervention would have had only nuisance value.

The Parliamentarian army, then, may have converged on Montgomery during 17 September in two or three columns, crossing the Camlad from the north by the Gaer bridge and possibly at the Salt bridge, and from the east, having crossed the Camlad near Chirbury, along the Chirbury to Caerhowel routeway.

This reconstruction of events assumes that Meldrum had not instead crossed the Severn after leaving Oswestry, and had taken the same route past Welshpool followed by Myddelton less than a fortnight earlier – marching south to re-cross the Severn at the Caerhowel bridge and so approaching Montgomery from the west. However, this seems an unlikely scenario as both armies would have been marching west of the Severn on near parallel routes, albeit with Byron's Royalists about half a day's march ahead and somewhat further to the west. Such a situation was likely to have resulted in an engagement before Montgomery was reached – although no such encounter is recorded. Had the Severn bridge at Caerhowel been that mentioned by Meldrum, this would position the Parliamentarians as either forcing a river crossing against the Royalist ranged on the east bank, an engagement that does not accord with the contemporary accounts, or else, had they gained a bridgehead on the east bank, fighting the battle on the narrow river plain near Caerhowel with their backs to the Severn and the Royalists having the advantage of the nearby high ground – an unfavourable position. Furthermore, if the Caerhowel bridge had been secured by the Parliamentarians on 17 September, this would mean that the Royalists had in turn abandoned a defensive river line position when they withdrew to the high ground above Montgomery.

Retreating from such a tactically advantageous position is difficult to explain. Furthermore, it seems odd that had the battle been fought near Caerhowel, why neither the Severn – a major navigable river and regional trade route – nor the bridge here, an important and well-known crossing place, were not accorded more attention in the contemporary accounts.

View southward towards Montgomery, from the possible Parliamentarian position near the farm at Stalloe (off camera to the right). The town lies on the skyline, on the lower slopes of the hill country surmounted by the now partly tree-covered Fridd Faldwyn, where the Royalist army camped the night before the battle.

A further argument militating against the battle having been fought near the Severn at Caerhowel is that positioned here Meldrum's army would have been almost two miles from Montgomery, separated from their comrades holding the castle by the intervening high ground occupied by the Royalist army. The contemporary accounts suggest that Meldrum boldly brought his army near to Montgomery. Taking position within site of the castle would have given encouragement to the garrison. The Parliamentarian correspondent Thomas Malbon even went so far as to say that the Parliamentarians had in fact relieved the castle on 17 September, the day before the battle. In a sense he may have been right, for although Meldrum's army seems not to have made actual contact with the garrison until after the battle, by positioning his army near the town on 17 September, causing the Royalists to withdraw to the high ground (and probably into the town also), Meldrum had in effect partly relieved the castle by clearing the enemy from the ground between it and his relieving army.

A more factually convincing reason to shift the site of the battle away from the Severn at Caerhowel is the lack of archaeological evidence. Almost all of the finds made by metal-detecting of debris associated with a Civil War battle site reported to date in the Montgomery area, including unused and fired ammunition, and other small finds relating to personal equipment and clothing, such as buckles and buttons, have been discovered in a north-north-westerly to due easterly arc within a mile of the town. The conclusion to be drawn from these accumulated finds – the product of professionally directed archaeological prospection, as well as discoveries reported by responsible hobby detectorists – is that the battle was fought on the still open farmland to the north and east of Montgomery.[8]

Given this scenario, if not at Caerhowel, where was the significant bridge? Of the two putative locations in the area, the County Boundary bridge and

---

8   Walters and Hunnisett, *The Civil War Battlefield at Montgomery*, pp. 6-12 and appended maps; Searches using *Archwilio: The Historic Environment Records of the Welsh Archaeological Trusts*. Available (summer 2015): www.archwilio.org.uk.

The river Camlad marks the northern limit of the battlefield area. A bridge mentioned in contemporary accounts of the battle may have stood near this spot.

the Salt bridge a bridge at the latter site seems more likely, although, as has been seen, the evidence remains equivocal. Sir John Meldrum's concern that the loss of the bridge would have endangered the Parliamentarian army's line of retreat is more understandable in the context of the Salt bridge site. Although finds of small arms ammunition discovered nearby show that fighting extended as far as the County Boundary bridge, had a bridge here been taken by the Royalists the Parliamentarians could still have conducted a withdrawal eastward in the Chirbury direction, making use of the Caerhowel to Chirbury routeway. The Royalist capture of a crossing of the Camlad at the Salt bridge, in the rear of the Parliamentarian army, would have been more significant. Such an outcome would have meant not only that the Parliamentarians had been outflanked, but also cut off from a northerly line of retreat across the Camlad. Meldrum would have been mindful that the bridge would assist a withdrawal of the army's supply train and artillery, and perhaps also the infantry, whose options for retreat would have been more limited than the mobile cavalry. While the Camlad today at about ten yards is not particularly wide, its banks are near vertical. Assuming that the river had a similar profile in the seventeenth century, it would have formed a dangerously disruptive obstacle for a retreating army.

Notwithstanding the hazard posed by the Camlad in the event of a retreat – and the river at the time of the battle was probably running deep, for there was considerable rainfall in this part of the Welsh borderlands during September 1644 – there is some opinion that the Parliamentarian army deployed on the river plain, with the Camlad immediately to its rear, and with the ditch and bank of the eighth-century earthwork known as Offa's Dyke protecting its left flank.

This, however, seems an unlikely position for several reasons. First, while the river would have covered the army's rear against a surprise attack from the north, a possible consideration for Meldrum, who may have expected the arrival of further Royalist reinforcements from that direction, and would protect against a wide outflanking manoeuvre, these advantages seem outweighed by the consideration that an ordered withdrawal or precipitate retreat by the Parliamentarians would be restricted and endangered by the course of the Camlad. Second, while the Offa's Dyke earthwork would have provided a defensible obstacle, by the seventeenth century it had been subject to centuries of erosion, and had in places been breached and lowered as a result of agricultural activity; so then, as now, the height of the bank and depth of the west-facing ditch would have varied considerably. The bank could have provided an elevated firing platform for a skirmish line of musketeers, but as a defensive position it would not lend itself to the usual firing by ranks practiced by the foot. The dyke would have also obstructed the Parliamentarians in the event of withdrawal or retreat. Furthermore, the right wing of the Royalist army advancing in a north-easterly direction could have crossed the dyke and so comprehensively outflanked the Parliamentarian left. Third, deployed on the Camlad's flood plain the Parliamentarians would have been without line of site to Montgomery Castle, their view obstructed by the first of a series of ridges forming the rising ground towards Montgomery. Besides, if the Royalists had occupied this ridge at the start of the battle it would have given them an advantageous position overlooking Meldrum's army. Fourth, no finds of debris associated with the battle having been fought on the river plain have been recorded (although this area has not, to date, been the focus of professional archaeological prospection by metal detection). Finally, Meldrum occupying a passive defensive position here at some distance from Montgomery does not seem to accord with the determined advance made by the Parliamentarian army towards the town on 17 September, causing the Royalists to withdraw, that the records indicate.

Given current evidence, then, it is most likely that the battle was fought within a mile to the north and east of Montgomery, with the armies engaged on a battlefront that could have stretched a mile or more: from the Hen Domen ridge to the north-west of the town, to the Lymore area to the east.

The topography here is sometimes described as a plain, although this is a misleading term to characterise a not entirely level landscape. The terrain becomes a true plain only near the Camlad. The town lies on the lower slopes of the hill country where the castle stands that fall away as a plateau towards the Camlad. To the north of Montgomery the plateau undulates as several distinct low ridges, lying roughly north-west to south-east. While not prominent from afar, when viewed on the ground these ridges are significant features in the landscape that could have provided the armies with advantageous positions for deployment. A ridge running south-east for about 550 yards from the farm at Stalloe, bounded to the east by the stream from Lymore and by another flowing in a hollow to the west of the County Boundary bridge, may have been the main position of the Parliamentarian foot. In view of the castle, this ridge, or another a little further south overlooking the Camlad plain, may also have been the position abandoned by the Royalists on the Parliamentarian approach. This was the overnight position of the Parliamentarian army, according to Sir Thomas Myddelton the 'field that was most advantageous for us'. The density of finds of battlefield debris located on the ridge at Ty-Ellen just 300 yards south of this putative Parliamentarian position provide evidence of combat and exchanges of fire in this area. A similar north-west to south-east ridge just outside the town may have been where the Royalists deployed at the beginning of the battle.

From the farm at Stalloe the land drops immediately to the Camlad flood plain, an area known as the Fflos. In the seventeenth century this was a tract of open meadowland that provided pasture owned in common for Montgomery's inhabitants. It is tempting to place much of the cavalry action in this area. Meldrum's description that part of the Royalist battle plan was 'to break through our forces, and to make themselves masters of a bridge we had gained the night before, which would have cut off the passage of our retreat', suggests that the bridge, although still guarded, rather than being closely defended as part of the Parliamentarian main position, was instead some way off and so vulnerable to a flanking manoeuvre. In the reconstruction proposed here, the main body of the Parliamentary horse was posted on the plain below the farm at Stalloe, forming the Parliamentarian right and securing an otherwise open flank while covering the Salt bridge half a mile or so to the rear.

In essence the battlefield has changed little since 1644. It remains an agricultural landscape with only scattered habitation. Modern Montgomery has not expanded far beyond the limits of the early Stuart town, that was itself still contained within the late medieval defences. The late Victorian Ordnance Survey mapping and an 1820 estate map, while depicting a field pattern around Montgomery similar to that of today, show a greater density of enclosure than at present. A widespread network of hedgerows similar to the nineteenth century field pattern across the seventeenth century landscape would have fragmented the battlefield, affecting deployment and manoeuvre. Land enclosure influenced the course of other Civil War battles – at first Newbury in September 1643, and at Nantwich in January 1644, for example. Fields and lanes bounded by hedgerows benefitted defensive action by infantry and limited offensive action by cavalry. On the other hand, when isolated from supporting cavalry and denied the defensive advantages of enclosed ground, infantry in open field country were vulnerable to flanking attacks and encirclement.

A schedule of rental due Lord Herbert from his estates around Montgomery dating from July 1642 provides an impression of the battlefield area.[9] It was then a more open agricultural landscape. The seventeenth century, with regional variations, was a period of increasing enclosure across much of England and lowland parts of Wales of the open or common field system that had characterised late medieval agriculture. Land enclosure was underway in Montgomeryshire by the time of the Civil War, but in summer 1642 the hinterland of Montgomery seems to have remained mainly an open field landscape. Lord Herbert owned much of the land here, but large tracts were kept in common by the town. There was a mixture of fields cultivated for arable, or given over to pasture for grazing and meadow for hay, dotted with isolated pockets of woodland. Something of the pattern and working of the open field system continued, with individuals cultivating 'ridges' of land – a survival of late medieval arable farming of strips of land within large shared fields. The enclosure of parcels of land does not seem to have been particularly widespread. There are few references to 'closes' – meaning hedged, fenced or walled plots – in Lord Herbert's schedule. Apart from the

---

9   NLW, Powis Castle Deeds and Documents, 1992.

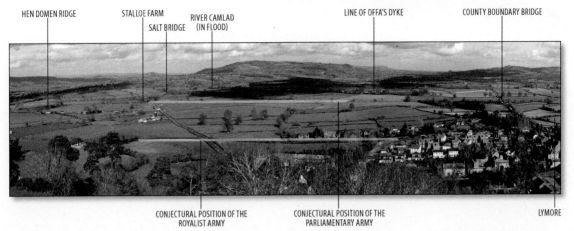

HEN DOMEN RIDGE   STALLOE FARM   RIVER CAMLAD   LINE OF OFFA'S DYKE   COUNTY BOUNDARY BRIDGE
                   SALT BRIDGE   (IN FLOOD)

CONJECTURAL POSITION OF THE   CONJECTURAL POSITION OF THE   LYMORE
ROYALIST ARMY   PARLIAMENTARY ARMY

Panorama of the probable battlefield area photographed from Montgomery Castle. (Courtesy of the Old Bell Museum, Montgomery. Photograph by Dr Martin Cadman)

town, the only other settlement in the battlefield area worthy of mention was the farm at Stalloe, a small estate in its own right, with an orchard, at least one close, and a watermill and feeder pool. To the east of Montgomery, in the Lymore area Lord Herbert had a country house or hunting lodge, known as the Black Hall, surrounded by fenced parkland where he kept deer and grazed his stable of horses. Herbert also kept deer on the 'mountain near the castle' – the open hilltop summit of Fridd Faldwyn.

The agricultural regime practiced at the time, then, does not seem to have determined the course of the battle. Indeed, none of the contemporary accounts mention difficulties posed by the terrain. There would have been relative freedom of manoeuvre across the mostly unenclosed fields, although tracts of cultivated land softened and muddied by recent rains would have impeded movement to some extent. Two watercourses in the area, that prior to eighteenth century and later agricultural improvement were more significant features in the landscape, may have affected deployment and manoeuvre: a stream flowing from a ravine to the north-west of Fridd Faldwyn, that in wet weather may have made boggy the fields at Sarkley, at the westerly end of the battlefield below the Hen Domen ridge; and the easterly stream flowing from the pools in the parkland at Lymore through the ravine now crossed by the County Boundary bridge. A little further northward near Rownal, in the late nineteenth century a ford was necessary to cross this stream, where today the flow of water is quite insignificant.

8

The battle of Montgomery

Sunrise on Wednesday 18 September 1644 found both armies positioned near Montgomery, the Royalists encamped on the hillsides around Fridd Faldwyn and among the siege lines facing the castle, and the Parliamentarians probably holding a ridgeline to the north-east of the town. The reason for the Royalist withdrawal to the high ground the previous day is unclear. Byron had perhaps only incompletely deployed his forces outside Montgomery when Meldrum's army, maybe approaching in columns from different directions, began to converge on the area. Unsure of the number of the enemy and mindful of the large garrison in the castle to their rear, Byron and his fellow officers may have considered it prudent to withdraw rather than risk an encounter engagement. Whether or not the Royalists also abandoned the town is again a matter for speculation. However, on the evening of 17 September the Parliamentary army was positioned within reach of the castle and had succeeded in unsettling the enemy.

It can be assumed that in both armies the senior commanders met that evening to discuss the situation, holding councils of war to determine the strategy for the coming day. Among the Royalists, Sir William Vaughan advocated quickly taking the offensive, and, according to Arthur Trevor, was 'the occasion of fighting the enemy in that place'. Byron and his officers, confident in their advantageous hilltop position, from where they may have noticed that they actually held numerical advantage, seem to have agreed with Vaughan to mount an all-out attack the next morning.

For their part, the Parliamentarian commanders adopted a more defensive plan, involving an attempt to resupply the garrison; as Sir Thomas Myddelton put it, 'We resolved not to go to them, but to endeavour the victualling of the castle'. While most of the army would remain in its overnight position, at first light cavalry would be dispersed to gather supplies of food and forage from the surrounding countryside. It may then have been envisaged that the horse would attempt to reach the garrison to off-load supplies. A similarly somewhat desperate re-supply action would be undertaken in Hampshire in November 1644, when a flying column of Royalist horse led by Sir Henry Gage managed to reach the beleaguered garrison holding Basing House. Gage 'was to have with him 1,000 horse, every one of which was to carry before him a bag or corn or other provisions […] and there [Basing] every trooper to cast down his bag; and then to make their retreat good as well they might'.[1]

Probably around first light on 18 September, then, about a third of the Parliamentarian horse dispersed as foraging parties. As a result, taking 'the advantage of the weakness of our quarters', as Meldrum later acknowledged, the Royalists prepared to attack. Their outposts may have reported groups of horse leaving the Parliamentarian lines, and daylight would have revealed both the limited number and isolated position of the enemy.

The Royalists came down steadily from the high ground and perhaps also through the town to deploy in good order on the outskirts of Montgomery, although probably coming under some harassing fire from the castle. Byron would have to have left a large contingent to occupy the siege lines to contain the garrison, and so his army forming battalia and preparing to engage the enemy may have numbered about 3,700 men. Thus at the beginning of the battle the Royalists enjoyed a significant numerical advantage over Meldrum's army, reduced by the temporary absence of the 500 or so foraging horse to less than 3,000.

Deployed in advance of the main line of the Royalist army was a 'forlorn hope' comprising dismounted dragoons, or detached, or 'commanded', parties of musketeers, led by an unnamed Dutch colonel. The purpose of a forlorn hope was to act in a skirmishing role, taking advantage of any cover to fire upon and test the enemy line, to delay them or perhaps provoke precipitate action. The Dutch colonel was, however, killed, and at that point the forlorn hope may have fallen back on the main body of advancing Royalist foot.

The entire Royalist line seems to have come forward in mounting a general attack; as Meldrum described it, 'Their horse and foot came on with great courage, resolving to break through our forces'. An objective of the Royalist cavalry may have been to outflank the Parliamentarian line and to threaten the Salt bridge, but they never reached that far. As a result the battle, as so often at the opening of other Civil War battles became a head on clash between the opposing lines of horse and foot. But unusually for the time, all or most of the cavalry was engaged only on one side of the battlefield, rather than on both opposing wings of the armies. This is confirmed by Arthur Trevor, in describing how 'the first charge [by the Royalist horse] was by my brother [Marcus Trevor's Regiment] upon all their horse, who killed Sir William Fairfax in the head of them and put them all in disorder'. Sir William Brereton acknowledged that 'our horse also at the beginning of the battle were worsted and retreated'. Some further explanation is required to explain how this may have come about.

Historians attempting to make sense of cavalry actions of the English Civil War, and indeed throughout military history, have tended to use language suggesting that the result of a determined charge by cavalry was physically, to deliver 'shock', or 'impact', or even to act as a 'missile' making a 'blow' against the enemy, without considering the outcome of such terms. Actual and deliberate collision has been seen as resulting from Civil War cavalry charges, at Naseby on 14 June 1645, for instance, where Prince Rupert's cavalry would rely on 'the sheer force of the impact', and later 'two bodies [of

---

1   Sir Edward Walker, *Historical Discourses upon Several Occasions* (London, 1705), p. 119.

horse] crashed into each other at sword point'.[2] Notwithstanding the natural instinct and inherent good sense of horses to avoid such impact by shying away from contact, the outcome of cavalry deliberately colliding in this way would be, as Keegan put it in similarly trying to make sense of Napoleonic cavalry charges, to 'achieve nothing but a collapsed scrimmage of damaged horses and men, growing bigger as succeeding ranks are carried on to the leading ones by their own impetus'.[3] Keegan went on to reconstruct the usual outcome of a clash between charging and counter-charging Napoleonic heavy cavalry – equipped and operating in a way not dissimilar to Civil War horse – prepared to receive and withstand the enemy. Advancing in order to maintain close order at the speed of a trot or canter, rather than in a hell-for-leather gallop, as the lines closed they slowed to a virtual halt as the riders pulled up to engage in a consensual melee, so that 'shock' action actually took the form of a sword fight. On the other hand, if one side turned and fled rather than face the enemy, the chargers then might spur on their horses to something more like a gallop, or 'a full career'; resulting in the sort of action as occurred outside Newark on 21 March 1644, when Parliamentary horse broke before Prince Rupert's Regiment, so that 'Sir Nicholas Crane charged quite through that body of rebels, pursuing them in rout'.[4]

The initial impetus of the Royalist horse at Montgomery led by Trevor's Regiment may have at first gained this sort of success, but although the outnumbered Parliamentarian horse were forced back, as a body they did not rout. Instead, as fresh squadrons on both sides were brought into action a general melee developed between often tightly packed horsemen using their swords and firearms at close range. This resultant press of horses and riders fighting at a standstill or at walking pace seems to have been typical of more sustained Civil War cavalry engagements, and matches earlier personal experiences of both Lord Byron and Oliver Cromwell. In the cavalry action at Gainsborough (Lincolnshire) on 31 July 1643, Cromwell found 'we disputed it with our swords and pistols a pretty time, all keeping close order, so that we could not break the other; at last they a little shrinking our men perceiving it, pressed in upon then and immediately routed the whole body'. Less than three weeks earlier, on 13 July, at the battle of Roundway Down (Wiltshire), Byron had fought in a similar cavalry engagement: 'So that first they gave us a volley of their carbines, then of their pistols, and then we fell in with them and gave them ours in the teeth, yet they would not quit their ground, but stood pushing it for a pretty space'.[5]

It was this pressing and pushing, the urging forward of their horses by individuals or groups of riders already engaged in hand-to-hand combat seeking to force and open gaps in the enemy line, then, that decided Civil War cavalry actions, rather than crashing lines of horsemen. This was the kind of prolonged cavalry melee that took place at Montgomery, in which

---

2   G. Foard, *Naseby The Decisive Campaign* (2nd edition, Barnsley, 2004), pp. 251-2.

3   J. Keegan, *The Face of Battle: A Study of Agincourt, Waterloo and The Somme* (Harmondsworth, 1976), p. 148.

4   Keegan, *The Face of Battle*, pp. 148-9; *Prince Rupert's Raising of the Siege at Newark Upon Trent*.

5   Rushworth, *Historical Collections*, Vol. 5, p. 278; *Sir John Byron's Relation to the Secretary of the Last Westerne Action between the Lord Willmot and Sir William Waller* (York, 1643).

Sir William Fairfax, far from being killed in the first charge, but like Marcus Trevor leading from the front, was first wounded, then captured, then rescued by his men, and then, having regrouped them, was more seriously wounded in leading the Yorkshire Horse to the attack once more. Trevor, too, was dismounted for a while when his favourite horse and charger for the day, a bay named Squire, was killed. However, in the ebb and flow of this sort of close fighting between horsemen well-protected by helmet, and buff coat or back and breast plate, there were probably many more wounds inflicted than actual fatalities; Fairfax's death later in the day was the result of the sum of the several wounds he had received.

Meanwhile, in the developing infantry battle the Royalist foot were at first as successful as the horse. Led by Colonels Robert Broughton and Henry Washington they advanced in good order towards the Parliamentarian line. In response, the Parliamentary foot almost immediately seem to have opened fire, but at too great a range to have much effect – probably at 200 yards or more. A report of the battle in a London newsbook that may have drawn on a first-hand Parliamentarian account, sheds some light on what happened: 'At the first advance of the enemy they [Meldrum's foot] discharged their muskets at too much distance, by reason of which our first impression failed of the execution which was expected. On this they with noise and violence pressed upon us and firing close upon our men they made them in some disorder to retreat'.[6] This statement indicates that the Parliamentary musketeers had fired by three-rank salvoes, in order quickly to deliver a weight of fire to bring the Royalist advance to a halt. This seems to have been a tactic used successfully by the Cheshire Foot in their recent engagements against Royalist horse at Oswestry, Ormskirk and Malpas, but on this occasion they had fired too soon. The Earl of Denbigh had commented that the Cheshire Foot were disengaged only after 'much difficulty' from the engagement on the western approaches to Shrewsbury on 4 July, and 'who could by no order be withdrawn from firing against the town'.[7] The fire control of Brereton's infantry had been wanting on that occasion, and having ineffectually delivered their opening salvoes *en masse* at Montgomery, fire from the Parliamentary line diminished as the musketeers hurriedly reloaded.

This gave the Royalist infantry the advantage of drawing near to deliver their fire at close range. Rather than giving fire by successive ranks, they too seem to have delivered at least one salvo, using what seems to have been an increasingly common tactic. During the second battle of Newbury, within six weeks of the battle of Montgomery, the Royalist foot 'after they had galled the rebels with several volleys, they fell on them with the butt end of their muskets'; and at Naseby, 'the foot on either side hardly saw each other until they were within carbine shot, and so only made one volley'.[8] The Royalist foot at Naseby then 'fell in with the sword and butt end of the musket'; a rapid advance after firing into hand to hand combat of the sort described by the 'noise and violence' of the Royalist attack that so disordered the Parliamentary line at Montgomery.

---

6   *The London Post*, 24 Sept. 1644.
7   *CSPD, 1644*, p. 338.
8   Walker, *Historical Discourses*, pp. 113, 130.

In places along the infantry battle front further exchanges of musketry fire may have continued at a distance, but elsewhere the lines closed and came to 'push of pike', while the musketeers engaged with their swords and reversed muskets. As Sir William Brereton described: 'It came to push of pike, wherein they were much too hard for us, having many more pikes'. Whether this was because of the Royalist infantry's numerical advantage, or, as seems more likely, because they had a higher proportion of pikemen to musketeers, the pike on this occasion had the advantage over firepower.

What actually occurred when two similarly determined pike blocks clashed has often been likened to a 'rugby scrum'.[9] However, to suggest that the way in which present-day re-enactors consensually raise their pikes to the vertical and then close *en masse,* to shove against each other shoulder-to-shoulder while leaning against their imitation pike shafts, surely bears little resemblance to the seventeenth-century reality. Instead, with their pikes 'charged', held horizontally at shoulder level in advancing upon the enemy, the push of the opposing pikemen was made in the earlier historical sense of the word, meaning to thrust or stab with a pointed weapon, especially a spear. This, of course, did not result in the mutual suicidal transfixion of the opposing front ranks, but rather in a form of fencing at spear point between the two lines about twenty feet apart, with the pike heads mostly clashing harmlessly at mid point. In this push by jabbing, causing some wounds but few immediate fatalities, pikes would be knocked down or up, and as men stepped forward or back, or stumbled or became fatigued, any gaps opening in the closely-packed ranks or any wavering of the line would be exploited by a determined enemy pushing forward. The resultant collapse of an enemy pike block was described by an officer of the Swedish army at the battle of Breitenfeld, fought near Leipzig on 7 September 1631, as 'when we might perceive their pikes and colours [i.e. the regimental company flags, kept among or alongside the pike blocks] to topple down, to tumble and fall cross one another: whereupon all his men beginning to flee, we had the pursuit of them'.[10]

There was, however, no similar rout of the Parliamentary foot at Montgomery. Although the Royalist salvoes and advantage at push of pike disordered the front ranks of Meldrum's line causing them to fall back in disorder, they rallied on what must have been a second supporting line of battalia near behind. Although Major James Lothian in particular among the senior officers was instrumental in rallying and re-ordering the Parliamentary lines, it was the steady morale, discipline and experience of the junior officers and rank and file that proved decisive at this point; as Meldrum expressed it, 'the resolution of the officers and soldiers of horse and foot'. In his opinion, 'the Cheshire Foot, with their officers', in particular, 'carried themselves more like lions than men'.

Nonetheless, at the turning point of the battle the Royalists seemed on the brink of victory. As one London journal, apparently drawing on another, rather confused, first or near second-hand account of the action put it, 'the enemy put by our pikes and the day seemed very doubtful, they being

---

9   For example by Barratt in *Cavaliers, The Royalist Army at War,* p. 45.

10   W. Watts, *The Swedish Discipline: The Third Part* (London, 1632), p. 65.

encouraged, crying "the day is ours, the day is ours".[11] Brereton agreed that 'We were so very hard tasked by the multitude of our enemies […] as that, if the commanders and soldiers had not engaged and behaved themselves very gallantly, or if we had wanted any part of our forces, it might have hazarded our army, for it was very dubious and uncertain which way the Lord would incline the victory'.

An assemblage of small arms ammunition recovered from the battlefield area. The spherical lead bullets are in different calibres for musket and carbine. The three lead slugs, or elongated shot, may have provided greater armour piercing or stopping power. Rather than being cast, these were hammered from a larger calibre bullet to fit a smaller bore weapon – typically a pistol. (Image courtesy of the Clwyd-Powys Archaeological Trust with the kind permission of the Trustees of the Lymore Estate)

It was the collapse of the Royalist horse that decisively turned the course of the battle. According to Arthur Trevor, 'all the Lancashire Horse' – probably including Byron's regiment, as well as those of Tyldesley and Molyneux – 'ran without a blow struck; which disheartened the foot so infinitely, that being in disorder with the pursuit of the enemy they could not be persuaded to rally again'. The Royalist horse had been unable to reinforce the success of the leading squadrons under Marcus Trevor's leadership. Perhaps difficult terrain affected deployment, while Arthur Trevor alluded to problems in command and control, in that Sir William Vaughan, despite having advocated taking the offensive, 'contributed not much to the action'. Morale may have been low among the Lancashire Horse in particular. The Parliamentarian horse, on the other hand, steadied after their initial set back and probably reinforced by the return of the foraging parties – which must have been urgently recalled when a general action appeared imminent – successfully counter-attacked. Although over simplifying and glorifying events, the aforementioned newsbook report seems to ring true in describing what then occurred: 'Sir Thomas Myddelton encouraged the horse, which were presently brought up again in a body (the Yorkshire Horse being commanded by Sir William Fairfax) charged the enemy with such valour and gallantry that their whole body were presently routed'.[12]

The sight of the flight of the previously unengaged Lancashire Horse, from what may have been a reserve position flanking their infantry, discouraged the nearest body of Royalist foot. This seems to have been Colonel Robert Ellice's small regiment, whose cowardice, according to Byron in a letter reflecting on the defeat written to Prince Rupert from Chester on 26 September, was the direct cause of his army's 'ill success'.[13] Ellice's men may have been left

---

11 *The Weekly Account*, 18-24 Sept. 1644.
12 Ibid.
13 BDL, Firth Manuscripts C7, folio 185.

exposed on a now open flank of the Royalist line. The Royalist foot had become disordered in following up as the Parliamentarian foot fell back. Threatened to the front by the re-ordered enemy infantry and outflanked by their horse, Ellice's Regiment broke and ran. This precipitated the general collapse of the Royalist foot in the face of a sweeping counter-attack by the steadier Parliamentarians; the 'one fresh gallant charge' described by Brereton. It is likely that by now the Parliamentary artillery had also come into action, and was inflicting casualties upon the Royalist foot at close range. Such a scenario may explain Meldrum's later uncharitable comment, believing he had been given too much credit for the victory, that Brereton had spent part of the battle 'standing by the cannon whilst others were in a fight, at a very far distance from any danger'.[14] Perhaps the artillery had been delayed in marching to Montgomery, so that Brereton busied himself in bringing it into action deployed among the supporting line of Parliamentary foot.

Confusion and panic spread rapidly throughout the Royalist army, as the brittle morale of units that had suffered recent defeats, and included many raw recruits, now gave way. As Arthur Trevor later wrote in disgust: 'Our men ran shamefully, when they had no cause of so great fear'. It was at this turning of the battle that the garrison of the castle, maybe having seen from their vantage point the retreat of the enemy horse, sallied forth and quickly overran the Royalists in their entrenchments, capturing many and breaking the siege. With most of their cavalry now fleeing or being pursued from the battlefield the Royalist foot soldiers either surrendered on the spot, or fled themselves in a state of what was then known as 'panic fear' – a result of battle fatigue and fright, compounded by the dismay and shock of defeat.[15] Ironically it was those men in the front ranks and centre, who had borne the brunt of the fighting, who had probably the best chance of their surrender being accepted. Their comrades on the flanks and in the rear of formations could more easily turn and run as panic fear spread, but were more likely to be cut down by the pursuing enemy. The Parliamentarian horsemen were said to have maintained their pursuit for about three miles from the battlefield, and it is was then, rather than during the battle itself, that most Royalists were killed.

Nonetheless, as at Naseby, a large proportion of the Royalist foot surrendered immediately *en masse*. Although the reported number of prisoners taken in the aftermath of the battle, most of whom were foot soldiers, varied considerably – Sir William Brereton, for example, thought there were 1,500 captives, while Sir John Meldrum numbered them at about 1,200 – probably upwards of 1,500 Royalists, including the walking wounded, were made prisoner of war. The lists of the officers taken named both major-generals, Colonel Robert Broughton and Sir Thomas Tyldesley; a Major Williams (probably of Richard Herbert's Regiment); an unidentified Lieutenant Colonel named Bladwell; nine captains; 17 lieutenants; a quarter master; three cornets of horse and 24 ensigns of foot; 52 sergeants; 55 corporals; and 11 drummers

---

14   *CSPD, 1644-1645*, pp. 5-6.
15   C. Carlton, *This Seat of Mars: War and The British Isles, 1485-1746* (New Haven and London, 2011), pp. 168-71

– 176 commissioned and non-commissioned officers in all.[16] The Parliamentarians gained 1,500 or as many as 2,000 weapons, depending on which report is accepted as fact, taken immediately or retrieved later from the battlefield and around the Royalist siege lines. The Royalists lost their transport, baggage and military supplies, including 20 barrels of gunpowder that had been delivered to Montgomery the day before.

A cast-iron solid round shot recovered from the battlefield area. Weighing about two pounds, this would have been fired from a type of light cannon known as a Falcon or Falconet. (Image courtesy of the Clwyd-Powys Archaeological Trust with the kind permission of the Trustees of the Lymore Estate)

Probably upwards of 400 Royalists were killed or died soon afterwards of wounds, with some reports suggesting that as any as 500 more were wounded; surely an exaggerated figure, probably confused and conflated with the number of walking wounded among the prisoners of war. However, even taking a conservative estimate, about half of the Royalist army became casualties or were captured.

The battle had lasted for only about an hour, although Lord Byron, attempting to put some gloss on an ignominious defeat, reckoned that 'it was more obstinately fought on both sides than any I have seen since the beginning of these wars'.[17] Post-battle Parliamentarian dispatches reported that Byron had immediately retreated to Shrewsbury with around 300 horse and some scattered foot, while Hunckes's Regiment of Foot and another body of horse also made their way there. So it appears that some Royalist units made a fighting retreat, or at least something of a orderly withdrawal from what was otherwise a Royalist debacle; summed up by a reflective Meldrum on 29 September, as 'the dissipating of the horse and total routing of the foot of that army'.[18] It is tempting to speculate that Lord Byron led the withdrawal of some units from the battlefield, as he had done after his similar defeat at Nantwich. But as with other aspects of Byron's direction of the battle, this remains a matter for speculation. Other reports suggest that Byron and Lord Molyneux made their way to Chester as soon as possible.

John Rushworth cited probably the most accurate casualty figures for the Parliamentarian army, in that they 'would not acknowledge above 60 or thereabouts on their side killed, and near 100 wounded'. 'Would not acknowledge' is a telling phrase, but it seems unlikely that Parliamentary

---

16 *Journals of the House of Lords*, Vol. 6, pp. 715-16.
17 BDL, Firth Manuscripts C7, folio 185.
18 *CSPD, 1644*, p. 543.

casualties were significantly greater, with the disproportionately higher Royalist casualty figures reflecting losses during the pursuit phase of the battle. The notable Parliamentary fatalities were Sir William Fairfax, dying of wounds, and a Major Fitzsimonds, who was Fairfax's deputy in command of the Yorkshire Horse. In a curious postscript to the battle, Sir John Meldrum threatened violence against the surgeons and orderlies who having unsuccessfully treated Sir William Fairfax then stole jewellery from his body. The incident was reported in a somewhat romanticised way in a London newsbook:

> Sir John Meldrum, who was so sensible of the loss of that brave commander Sir William Fairfax and that the affliction would be great to his wife (as indeed it was sad to the kingdom), that he procured from among the soldiers or surgeons (not without some difficulty) the diamond ring that was on his finger, and the bracelet of gold that was about his arm and sent it up to his lady with a letter […]: And that when these things were denied him by some surgeons and also by others (unexpected) claiming them to be their due, he drew up some horse and said, he would deal with them as with enemies if they did not deliver the same to be sent to his lady.[19]

---

19 *The Kingdomes Weekly Intelligencer*, 24 Sept-1 Oct. 1644.

9

Aftermath and impact

The battle of Montgomery was a clear-cut Parliamentarian victory. While achieving their twin objectives of relieving the garrison of the castle and securing the munitions taken at Newtown, they had also shattered the regional Royalist field army. The resilience of the Parliamentarian army and the effectiveness of its leadership were the factors that had most determined the outcome of the battle. Sir John Meldrum in his dispatch to the Committee of Both Kingdoms written next day, confidently reported:

> That, by the blow given here, the best of their foot are taken away; Shrewsbury, Chester, and Liverpool, unfurnished with ammunition; and North Wales (which formerly hath been the nursery for the King's armies) in all likelihood will shake off that yoke of servitude which formerly did lie upon their neck, and will be reduced to the obedience of King and Parliament, by the example of Montgomery Castle.[1]

At the Royalist headquarters at Shrewsbury the same day, Sir Michael Ernle penned a gloomy situation report to Prince Rupert. While Sir William Vaughan and Sir Thomas Dallison had safely returned to Shrewsbury late on the 18th, presumably after having tried to rally their horsemen, neither could confirm the true scale of the defeat. 'Which I fear is very great', wrote Ernle, 'for there is very few of out foot come in'. 'This country is now in bad condition […] in danger to be lost'.[2]

At Montgomery, local Parliamentary supporters, and perhaps also fair weather Royalists recognising a shift in the balance of power, began to arrive there in the afternoon and evening of the battle to make themselves known to Sir Thomas Myddelton. Foremost among them was the MP Sir John Price, who in fact seems to have joined Myddelton at Montgomery in early September and had remained at the castle during the siege.

Meldrum, meanwhile, soon found that his most pressing problem was what to do with the 1,500 prisoners of war, who by his reckoning were outnumbered by the rank and file of the Parliamentary foot by only about 100 men. The major generals Broughton and Tyldesley would be held captive,

---

1   *Journals of the House of Lords*, Vol. 6, p. 715.
2   BL, Additional Manuscripts 18981, folio 253.

The fighting during September 1644 caused little damage to Montgomery. Several buildings in the modern town survive from that time, like that pictured above in Arthur Street.

along with probably the majority of the commissioned officers, but detaining and providing for hundreds of NCOs and rank and file was an insurmountable problem. Brereton proposed that those prepared to take an oath of allegiance to Parliament could be shipped from Liverpool, once it was taken, to fight the Royalists and Catholic rebels in Ireland, but this seems an improbable outcome. Reenlistment with the victors among the common soldiers of a defeated force became a regular occurrence as the Civil War went on, and so many Royalists may indeed have joined the Parliamentarians. Others were probably released on parole, and either deserted or eventually rejoined their units. Four Parliamentarian deserters found among the Royalist prisoners, however, were taken to Nantwich, and after trial by a council of war, were found guilty of running from their colours to the enemy and executed on 25 September.[3]

The difficulty of securing and providing for the prisoners only compounded the problems already besetting Meldrum's hastily formed field army. It had marched quickly to Montgomery but with little logistical support, and this was now felt. The rank and file, far from their usual bases and sources of pay and supplies, expressed their 'grudging and discontentment'. They became mutinous and the prisoners of war angry because of the lack of bread. Sir Thomas Myddelton and the Shropshire committee at Wem hurriedly had to scrape together £600 in emergency payment to the Yorkshire Horse. The Parliamentarians had considered launching an attack on Shrewsbury, but optimistic reassurances given by Myddelton and some of the Shropshire Parliamentarians that sympathisers in the town would rise against the weakened garrison if Meldrum's army made its way there proved unrealistic. Within days of the battle the Parliamentarian army began to return northward. Leaving Myddelton at Montgomery with his own men and a couple of troops of Brereton's Regiment to help bring in supplies,

---

3   Malbon, 'Memorials of the Civil War', p. 147.

Meldrum and Brereton had returned to Oswestry in Shropshire by 21 September.

There, Meldrum ruled out any further offensive. Writing to update the Committee of Both Kingdoms, he expressed his concern that the continued bad weather would hamper further operations, and represented the unlikelihood of successfully being able to assault Shrewsbury, 'as by the scanty intelligence we had'. Exaggerating for effect the strength of Shrewsbury's fortifications as being 'the strongest works in England', Meldrum felt he had too few men to launch a determined assault, let alone maintain a siege, while simultaneously guarding the large number of prisoners led from Montgomery. The army was becoming disorderly, especially the Yorkshire Horse, and many soldiers were doing 'nothing but rob and spoil the country, which cannot be prevented so long as they have nothing to maintain themselves'. A proposal to attack Bridgnorth instead was considered but rejected, and Meldrum was by now concerned with achieving more certain success by returning to the siege of Liverpool. By 29 September he had reached Warrington in Cheshire near the border with Lancashire. He planned to cooperate with Brereton and the Lancashire county forces to put further pressure on Chester and to take Liverpool, which eventually surrendered to him on 1 November. [4]

Meanwhile Lord Herbert, taking advantage of the Parliamentary withdrawal and the availability of an armed escort, left Montgomery, and via the Parliamentary bases at Stafford and Coventry travelled to London to make his peace with Parliament. Herbert's tenants and the other inhabitants of Montgomery set about assessing their losses, in property harmed and provisions and provender taken during the military occupation. The aldermen later reckoned that the town's cumulative damages, 'by the King's army under the command of Colonel Broughton and of the losses and damnifications [sic] of the Parliament army under Sir Thomas Myddelton', came to £3,066 – upwards of half a million pounds in today's terms. [5]

Established in his new base at Montgomery, Myddelton reflected on 'as great a victory as hath been gained in any part of the kingdom', but requested reinforcements from the Committee of Both Kingdoms and forewarned them that he saw little hope of financing his war effort from local taxation. He had found it difficult to pay his own men, let alone to subsidise Meldrum's soldiers. Nonetheless, Myddelton was able to secure Newtown and also began to attract new recruits, having given a colonel's commission to Sir John Price to raise a regiment of foot. It would, however, be some time before they were of much use. 'I dare not trust to my own countrymen who are newly raised', he reported to London on 12 October, 'either to keep the garrisons or to go upon any design'. [6]

By then, however, Myddelton had already taken the offensive by capturing the Red Castle, the Royalist base that had been a thorn in his side since commencing operations in Montgomeryshire. The Parliamentarians occupied Welshpool on the last day of September, where Myddelton extended his recruitment drive by issuing a proclamation, calling on all men in the area

---

4   *CSPD, 1644,* pp. 505, 524, 543-4; *CSPD, 1644-1645,* pp. 5-6.
5   NLW, Herbert Manuscripts and Papers, Series II, Vol. IX, E6/1, folio 42.
6   *CSPD, 1644-1645,* p. 34.

Powis Castle (in the seventeenth century known as the Red Castle), a Royalist garrison stormed and captured by Sir Thomas Myddelton's brigade on 2 October 1644.

aged between 16 and 60 who were physically fit for military service to join him. Once again employing the tactic of attacking under cover of darkness, on the early morning of 2 October Myddelton assaulted the castle with most of his brigade – 400 foot and 50 horse. With the horse and 100 foot posted as a rearguard, the rest of the infantry in three companies deployed around the castle and opened fire to distract the garrison and cover the assault party. While the use of a petard had been threatened against Montgomery Castle, on this occasion John Arundel, Myddelton's engineer and master gunner, deployed one to actual effect. The petard successfully blew apart the outer gate, and the assault party entered the castle. Although at first the garrison resisted, they hurriedly surrendered when the Parliamentarians also forced their way into the inner ward. Nearly 100 Royalists, including Lord Powis, were taken prisoner, along with 200 weapons and 40 horses – most of them from a 25-strong troop that had arrived as reinforcements just a few days earlier. Myddelton admitted one fatality among his men during an action lasting for less than an hour.[7]

In mid-October Myddelton launched a raid into south-west Shropshire, causing the Royalists to abandon an outpost near Bishop's Castle, and at the end of the month again joined forces with his brother in law Colonel Mytton in mounting a larger raid against the garrison of Ruthin. In December Myddelton struck south and stormed the Royalist garrison at Abbey Cwmhir in Radnorshire, and for a short while over Christmas laid unsuccessful siege to his own home at Chirk Castle, by attempting to undermine a section of the walls.

By the end of 1644 Myddelton had established and successfully held a Parliamentarian enclave in mid-Wales centred on his garrisons at Montgomery and Welshpool. A county committee for Montgomeryshire based at the Red Castle was set up in opposition to what was left of the local Royalist administration. But Myddelton was relatively isolated. Logistics remained problematic – in November, for instance, a Liverpool-bound ship chartered to carry arms and 50 barrells of gunpowder from London foundered in the Irish Sea – and although he received some small reinforcements, his brigade continued to suffer badly from desertion. As a result, Myddelton always

---

7   Ibid., p. 3; BL, Additional Manuscripts 18981, folio 281.

lacked strength in men and military supplies to take the offensive further into Wales and to gain fresh territory. At the close of 1644, the war in the Principality and its borderlands was not a priority for the Committee of Both Kingdoms, while Sir William Brereton, the most powerful Parliamentary leader in the region, was directing most of his resources against Royalist Chester.

On the Royalist side, Lord Byron put a brave face on the defeat. In reporting to Prince Rupert on 26 September, after accusing Ellice's Regiment of cowardice, Byron reckoned that the enemy had been so damaged by the battle, 'that they are not able to attempt the siege of any of our towns', but admitted, 'that by being masters of the field they so cut off our contributions' (i.e. levies in cash or provisions in kind demanded from the civilian population). Fearing the damage to his reputation, Byron hoped from his patron that 'I may not suffer any prejudices in you highnesses good opinion (which I value above all things) through malicious relations of my actions here. No man, I am sure, can carry a more faithful heart to your highness's service'.[8] Byron was of course right that he would be blamed. Arthur Trevor, reporting to the Marquis of Ormonde, accused Byron of having wasted Ormonde's valuable reinforcements, and condemned him for having supplanted Lord Capel's command in the first place. At Chester in November, Byron and the city's governor Major Will Legge were reportedly still at loggerheads, Legge accusing Byron of having caused the defeat at Montgomery, while Byron in turn blamed Legge for the loss of Liverpool.[9]

To John Williams, the Archbishop of York, at Conway, his hometown and fastness on the north Caernarvonshire coast, which he had fortified since returning there in 1642 to uphold the Royalist war effort in north-west Wales, the debacle at Montgomery had a worse effect than the Royalist losses in Yorkshire resulting from the battle of Marston Moor.[10] Although the defeat of Prince Rupert's Welsh borderlands army and of the Marquess of Newcastle's Northern Army at Marston Moor was on a greater scale to that of Lord Byron's army at Montgomery, in regional terms Williams was correct. As in Yorkshire, the Royalists had lost the capacity for offensive action and had retreated to their garrisons. Byron's view that the enemy lacked resources to besiege the larger Royalist bases in the region was correct, but also showed how Montgomery had forced the King's forces onto the defensive. After the defeat Sir Michael Ernle hurriedly had to reinforce existing or establish new garrisons in west Shropshire in what had become a new front. Byron undertook little further offensive action during the remainder of the war, being restricted by the enemy to defend Chester until he surrendered the city in February 1646.

It was also hard for the Royalists to make good their losses in men and arms at Montgomery. The majority of the horse had escaped the battle, and many foot probably also eventually rallied to their colours, but it would take time to reform these units and for them to regain combat effectiveness. Recruitment in Wales, as Prince Rupert had found in August, had become

---

8   BDL, Firth Manuscripts C7, folio 185.
9   *CSPD, 1644-1645,* p. 34.
10   Phillips, *Civil War in Wales and the Marches,* Vol. 2, p. 215.

increasingly unsustainable. Myddelton's Parliamentary enclave in the midst of what since 1642 had been the so-called 'nursery' of the King's infantry can only have made Royalist recruitment more problematic. However, it is doubtful that the permanent loss to the Royalist armies of perhaps 1,600 soldiers, because of death, incapacitating wounds, desertion or side-shifting, as a consequence of the battle of Montgomery had a significant effect on the outcome of the campaigns in 1645.

The Royalists would, however, have found it difficult quickly to replace the arms and munitions lost at Montgomery, particularly as Myddelton's garrisons threatened their already over extended and vulnerable supply lines.

For Royalism in the region the defeat at Montgomery was as much a psychological as a damaging military blow. It unnerved the King's supporters and heartened his opponents in a part of the kingdom that until then had been seen as reliably Royalist. 'Since our late disaster at Montgomery the face of our condition is much altered', wrote Sir Michael Ernle to Prince Rupert on 2 October, the day that unbeknown to him Myddelton had taken the Red Castle: 'The edge of the gentry is very much abated, so that they are all at a stand and move but heavily to advance this service. The countryside's loyalty is strangely weakened, they begin to warp to the enemy'. At Ludlow, Sir Michael Woodhouse upheld this gloomy outlook, reporting to Rupert three days later: 'Since my last letters presented to your highness of the loss and ill success of Montgomery, we have no appearance of an alteration for the better'.[11] While gentry support in Shropshire and elsewhere in the region faltered, the Royalist administration encountered widespread reluctance to pay military taxes and to cooperate with the garrisons. Sir John Menes was a Royal Navy captain turned professional soldier, who earlier in 1644 had been sent by Prince Rupert to superintend the Royalist war effort in North Wales, and had since established himself as the Prince's viceroy at Beaumaris on the Isle of Anglesey. Later in October, Mennes reckoned that the loss at Montgomery and of the Red Castle had caused Montgomeryshire to revolt, and that civilian discontent and Parliamentary activism had also spread into neighbouring Merionethshire.[12]

Animosity to the authority of the Royalist military because of the loss of its repute, and the unsettling of Royalist popular support were consequences of the battle of Montgomery. Both outcomes encouraged the emergence of two movements that towards the end of 1644 and into the New Year for a while destabilised and threatened the Royalist war effort across the region: the Marcher Association and the Clubmen. The Marcher Association was an uneasy gentry-led alliance, of anxious loyal and also discontented Royalists joined by militant neutralists, across Shropshire, Herefordshire, Worcestershire and Staffordshire that sought greater control over the war effort, including raising its own militias. The so-called Clubmen were a more spontaneous vigilante movement of armed civilians, active mainly in Herefordshire and south Shropshire, but also elsewhere in the mid borderlands of Wales, who for a while were openly antagonistic to the Royalist military.

---

11 BDL, Firth Manuscripts C7, folio 191; BL, Additional Manuscripts 18981, folio 284.
12 BDL, Firth Manuscripts C7, folio 205.

While not a marking a pivotal turning point in the First English Civil War, then, the battle of Montgomery and the resultant Parliamentarian inroads into mid-Wales destabilised one of the few remaining Royalist heartlands. This did not create an irrecoverable situation for King Charles, but made it far more difficult for his forces in the decisive year of 1645 to turn the war in his favour.

A final postscript to the battle was the destruction of Montgomery Castle. It remained a Parliamentary garrison until after the end of the First Civil War, apart from a short spell around May 1645 when Sir John Price, then acting as governor, once again sensed a change in the fortunes of war and briefly side-shifted to the King. Upon the death of Edward Lord Herbert in August 1648, Richard Herbert inherited his father's title, becoming second Baron Herbert of Cherbury. Heavily fined by Parliament as punishment for having so actively supporting the King, because of Parliament's postwar policy of 'slighting' – rendering indefensible by demolition castles or other buildings that had, or might serve as rallying points for Royalist resistance – Richard also had to comply with a directive to destroy the castle. The Parliamentary county committee for Montgomeryshire oversaw the demolition, which was undertaken in a systematic way, so that proceeds from the sale of salvaged materials could be taken in part payment of Richard's fines. The demolition of Montgomery Castle began in June 1649 and was completed that November. The work was so thoroughgoing that just foundations and fragmentary upstanding masonry remained. The salvaged materials, reclaimed mostly from the New Castle, including bricks and roof tiles, and the decorative timber wainscoting that had once clad the walls of Lord Edward Herbert's fine apartments, were valued at £500.[13]

---

13 NLW, Herbert Manuscripts and Papers, Series II, Vol. IX, E6/1, folios 21, 24, 30. This was a substantial sum, when at the time an unskilled casual, or day, labourer would do well to earn about £10 in a year.

Colour Plate Commentaries

Plate C
Royalist soldiers of the Anglo-Irish Foot

This interpretation represents soldiers from the regiments of the English army in Ireland that, as a result of the ceasefire, or 'Cessation', agreed in September 1643 in the concurrent war with the Catholic Irish Confederacy, from late autumn 1643 into spring 1644 were shipped from Munster and Leinster to join Royalist forces in the English West Country and about north-east Wales and Chester. Royalists eagerly anticipated this reinforcement, in part to counter the expected invasion of northern England by Scottish Covenanter forces as a result of the Solemn League and Covenant with Parliament also agreed in September 1643. As Arthur Trevor, agent on the British mainland to the Duke of Ormonde, commander-in-chief of the army in Ireland, reported to his patron from Oxford in later November 1643 (when in fact advance units of the expeditionary force had already landed in north-east Wales), 'The expectation of the English-Irish aid is the daily prayers, and almost the daily bread of them that love the King and his business; and is put into the dispensary and medicine book of state as a cure for the Scotch'.[1]

However, because of the acute shortage of clothing, military supplies and pay by then besetting the army in Ireland, compounded by the hardships experienced by the soldiers on campaign, in early November Ormonde had forewarned the Royalist authorities that upon the arrival of his veteran Leinster-based troops it would be necessary:

> That all possible provision be made for the good entertainment of the officers and soldiers, who are in the greatest want that can be imagined, and in such distemper by reason thereof, that I much fear great inconveniences will unavoidably fall upon the King's service, if they find not their condition much mended upon the instant of their landing.[2]

To pay, clothe and feed the Anglo-Irish reinforcement in the North Wales region would require huge administrative and logistical Royalist effort. But such 'provision' for the soldiers was obtained, largely as a result of the energetic direction of the leading Chester Royalist Orlando Bridgeman, who galvanised into activity the Royalist civilian authorities of the northerly Welsh counties and of the City of Chester and its hinterland. At the end of

---

1   Carte, *A Collection of Letters, Written by the Kings Charles I and II*, p. 208.
2   Ibid., p. 198.

November 1643, writing from Beaumaris on the Royalist Isle of Anglesey in north-west Wales, Bridgeman was confidently able to report to Ormonde that:

> Now your forces are at Chester, where we endeavour all that is possible for their accommodation […]. I have provided shoes and stockings for 1,000 or 1,200 of them already delivered, and the rest were in making, which I hope they have by this time. I have gotten cloth and frieze [coarse woollen cloth, a staple product of mid and north Wales] sufficient for them all, not yet made into apparel, but hastened into Chester, where I hope to have it fitted up this week and the next. And I am now purposely in these parts to raise some proportion of money for the officers and soldiers, and have gotten about £1,000, which I shall distribute with their advice to the best advantage of his Majesty's service.[3]

At first some of the soldiers were given donated or requisitioned civilian clothing, and the sergeant at the left of the group here wears a canvas doublet. His headwear is a workaday knitted woollen full-brimmed hat, popularly worn since the sixteenth century, known as a 'Statute cap'. His military status is, however, clearly displayed by his halberd, a type of polearm indicating the rank of sergeant. As well as wielding the weapon in close-quarter fighting, sergeants used their halberd during drill or in combat to direct the soldiers to maintain formation. As the contemporary military theoretician Richard Elton remarked: 'Perceiving any soldier out of order, he may cast in his halberd between their ranks to cause him to march even abreast'.

The musketeer to the sergeant's left playing dice on the drumhead wears a collar, or bandolier, of charges. These cylindrical gunpowder holders reconstructed here instead of wooden have pewter caps, a metallic fitting often found in archaeological research on the sites of civil war engagements and strongholds. Each powder holder was suspended from the bandolier by a looping string passing through and securing the two cap lugs and both lugs on the container, so that once opened cap and holder could not be dropped. Units on both sides wore red coats before Parliament adopted the colour for the uniforms of the foot soldiers of the New Model Army in 1645 (see also Plate F). The Royalist redcoat interpreted here wears a commonplace woollen hat (see also Plate E), usually referred to as a Monmouth cap. (Photo: Charles Singleton/Interpreters, L-R: Steve Stanley, Simon Frame, Spencer Houghton)

Plate D
The cavalry mêlée at the height of the battle of Montgomery, 18 September 1644

This reconstruction interprets the confused close-quarter fighting that ensued in a civil war cavalry engagement when, rather than recoil or retreat, both sides determinedly advanced into contact. In the foreground the Royalist colonel of horse Marcus Trevor desperately defends himself after being unhorsed from his mortally wounded charger. Rescued and remounted on a fresh horse, Trevor survived the battle, and on his return to Chester related his experience to his brother, who wrote: 'what horse

---

3   Ibid., p. 211.

was lost in the action were out of my brother's regiment, and not many; but among them his jewel bay, Squire, whose solemn mourner he now is'. Horses were more vulnerable than their well-equipped riders, and the majority of the horsemen depicted here are outfitted in the full protective kit of a medium cavalryman, or 'harquebusier', of a buff coat worn under steel back and breast plate, and the so-called 'lobster pott' helmet, the ubiquitous head piece of civil war cavalry. While most of the cavalry regiments on both sides at Montgomery were experienced or even veteran units, and so it can be assumed that by this stage of the war the officers and troopers would have been well equipped, either by general issue or by personal acquisition, it is uncertain whether the breast and back plate were commonly worn in addition to a buff coat. Troopers in particular may more often have worn a buff coat, or back and breast plate, rather than both. While the sword was the cavalryman's main weapon in close-quarter fighting, other arms were also deployed. The Parliamentarian trooper confronting Colonel Trevor having fired one of his pistols aggressively hurls it at the Royalist, for it was both difficult and dangerous to attempt to reload firearms with the enemy so close. In the background a Royalist wields a pollaxe, an effective cutting and piercing hand weapon advocated by the contemporary military theoretician John Vernon: 'A poll axe is very necessary for a trooper […] where your sword can do no good but little execution, your poll axe may be an advantage unto you to offend your enemy'. (Illustration by Maksim Borisov, © Helion & Company Limited)

Plate E

Rank and file foot soldiers of the Royalist army

A musketeer of Colonel Henry Tillier's Regiment of Foot readies his matchlock musket for action. He keeps alight the smouldering end, or 'coals', of the match cord, which when the trigger was pulled stubbed into the gunpowder in the musket's priming pan to ignite the main charge in the breech. Looped around his collar of bandoliers is a spare bundle of match. Because the cord had to be kept lit well before and during action civil war armies consumed match in prodigious quantities. Identified by the Royalist cavalry officer and diarist Richard Symonds as 'foot greencoates [sic]', Tillier's was one of the so-called 'English-Irish' regiments from the English army in Leinster shipped to the North Wales region in later 1643 and early 1644. That green was the regiment's distinguishing uniform colour is confirmed in the Royalist Colonel Dallison's dispatch written to Prince Rupert at Welshpool in early August 1644, mentioning that local and regional clothworkers had manufactured 'coats and caps for foot soldiers […] an 100 of which are blue, which will serve very well for your Highnesses regiment of foot. The rest are green, which may serve for Colonel Tilliers'. Rather than having been issued with one of these new green cloth caps (probably made in the Montero style), however, this musketeer wears a simple workaday knitted woollen cap in civilian fashion. Probably often having a high conical shape, this form of popular headwear seems to have been generally known as a Monmouth cap. A notable production centre for such caps was Bewdley, a small town on the River Severn in south-west Worcestershire, Royalist territory when Richard Symonds's unit passed through there in mid-June 1644. As Symonds described: 'the only manufacture of this town is making of caps called Monmouth caps. Knitted by poor people for 2d. [two pennies] a piece, ordinary ones sold for 1s. [one shilling, equal to 12 pennies], 3s., 4s. First they are knit, then they mill them, then block them, then they work them with tassels, then they sheer them'.

The central figure is a pikeman of the Shropshire Trained Bands, the county militia regiment. His equipment is based on kit inspections of the Ludlow town detachment mentioned in musters lists spanning the decade prior to the outbreak of civil war. These records document concerted efforts made to equip the trained soldiers from Ludlow with up to date arms and armour. This militiaman wears full pikeman's armour, a panoply known as a corselet, comprising a back and breast plate, attached tassets to protect the upper legs and groin area, and a pikeman's helmet, or pott, of an English pattern manufactured about 1635. Both helmet and armour are 'russetted'. Russetting was a controlled surface rusting treatment, involving the application of an acidic solution such as vinegar or urine, done to resist further oxidation and thus actual corrosion of the metal. He also wears a sword described in the Ludlow muster book, as often elsewhere in contemporary records, simply as a 'tuck'; a stout standard mass-produced sword with a simple hilt.

Next to the trained bandsman is a more lightly equipped pikeman of Colonel Michael Woodhouse's Regiment of Foot, a bluecoat unit also based at Ludlow in south Shropshire as the permanent garrison there. (Illustration by Maksim Borisov, © Helion & Company Limited)

Plate F
Rank and file foot soldiers of the Parliamentary army.
The musketeer is from Sir Thomas Myddelton's Brigade, either of his own regiment of foot, or that of his cousin, Sir William Myddelton. A record from early October 1644 of payment for making soldiers' coats from red cloth indicates that this was the uniform colour of one or both of these regiments. In addition to their firearm, Myddelton's musketeers were issued with a sword, here worn from a buff leather baldric; with a collar of bandoliers – a leather belt with an attached bullet pouch from which hung by strings a number of turned wooden containers, each holding a measured charge of gunpowder for a single shot, and a separate container holding priming powder; and with a 'snapsack', a leather haversack or satchel, depicted here slung over the right shoulder, holding rations and the soldier's personal effects. In March 1644 one James Goffe, a London-based manufacturer of leather-ware, was paid for supplying 300 such snapsacks to Myddelton's Brigade. This soldier is armed with a flintlock musket, generically known at the time as a firelock or as a snaphance; the latter term was also used then, as today, to define a particularly English design of firing mechanism. While the matchlock was the standard infantry firearm of the period, a significant number of Sir Thomas Myddelton's musketeers were equipped with flintlocks. For example, on 2 September 1644, on the eve of the Montgomery campaign, Captain Elliott's company of foot was issued with 12 new snaphances, while fellow-Captain Roger Bromfield's company received 32 firelocks.

Beside the musketeer is a pikeman of Colonel Simon Rugeley's Regiment of Foot, a grey-coated unit from the Staffordshire county forces. As a secondary weapon he also wears a sword, suspended from a waist-belt and hanger, and over his shoulder is slung a snapsack similar in design to a modern duffle bag. His headwear is a practical peaked cap made of woollen cloth, interpreted today and probably known then as a Montero. A skirt around the edge of the cap also forming the peak could be folded down for protection against inclement weather. (Illustration by Maksim Borisov, © Helion & Company Limited)

Plate G
A cornet of horse of the Parliamentary army.

Cornet was both the most junior commissioned rank in the cavalry and the name given to the standard that these officers were entrusted with carrying. The subaltern pictured here is from Sir Thomas Myddelton's own regiment of horse. The cornet itself was the troop captain's personal standard identifying the unit. It was flown from a wooden lance, depicted here with a carrying handle in addition to the handgrip. The heraldic devices and other imagery, and accompanying text, written as slogans or mottos, often, as here, in Latin script, displayed on these banners expressed the commanding officer's allegiance and motivation for taking up arms. Myddelton's own motto, displayed in scrollwork on a green field, indicates his belief in the righteousness of the Parliamentary cause: 'In Veritate Triumpho' approximately translating into English as 'I triumph in the truth'. After the civil wars this would remain the motto of successive generations of the Myddelton family.

The design of the cornet would most likely have been hand painted onto green taffeta (a lustrous silk or silk-like material). It was probably made in London by one Mr Sedgewick, a tradesman who in April 1644 received payment for providing a similar banner for Captain Ellice, one of Myddelton's troop commanders. That also had fringing and cords and tassels in green and white, and Sedgewick charged 14 shillings for designing (probably including painting) the cornet.

The cornet himself under a long riding coat wears the ubiquitous protective 'buff coat'. Tough enough to turn a sword blade yet flexible, and weather resistant, with or without sleeves these deep-skirted doublets were made from buff leather, usually cattle hide tanned with oil. Ochre added during the tanning process gave the coats a distinctive yellowish colour. The cornet wears his sword from a baldric slung over the right shoulder. His headwear is a cloth Montero cap, which he is likely to have changed for a steel pott helmet when going into action. (Illustration by Maksim Borisov, © Helion & Company Limited)

Bibliography

Manuscript Sources

Aberystwyth, **The National Library of Wales**
Chirk Castle Manuscripts and Estate Records.
Herbert Manuscripts and Papers.
Powis Castle Deeds and Documents.
Sweeney Hall Manuscripts.
Llandrindod Wells, **Powys Archives**
Montgomeryshire Quarter Sessions Records.
London, **The British Library**
Additional Manuscripts 18981, Prince Rupert's Papers.
London, **The National Archives**
SP28, Commonwealth Exchequer Papers.
SP84/86, State Papers Foreign, Holland.
Oxford, **The Bodleian Library**
Dugdale Manuscripts 19, Docket Book of the Clerks of Chancery at Oxford, 1643-6.
Firth Manuscripts C6-7, Transcripts of Prince Rupert's Papers.
Tanner Manuscripts 57, The Clerk of Parliament's Papers.
Shrewsbury, **Shropshire Archives**
Bridgnorth Corporation Collection.
Stafford, **William Salt Library**
Prince Rupert's Papers.

Published Primary Sources
Published in London, unless otherwise stated.

(i) Contemporary Tracts and Pamphlets
Cheshire's success since their pious and truly valiant colonel Sir William Brereton, baronet, came to their rescue (Undated, 1643).
Sir John Byron's Relation to the Secretary of the Last Westerne Action between the Lord Willmot and Sir William Waller (Undated, York, 1643).
A True and Exact Relation of the Great Victories Obtained by the Earl of Manchester and The Lord Fairfax Against the Earl of Newcastle's Army in the North (October 1643).
His Highness Prince Rupert's Raising of the Siege at Newark Upon Trent, 21 March 1644 (Oxford, April 1644).
Two Great Victories: On[e] Obtained by the Earle of Denbigh at Oswestry […] The Other by Colonel Mitton (June 1644).
A Copy of A Letter sent From Sir Tho. Middleton, to the Honourable, William Lenthall Esq; Speaker of the House of the House of Commons. Concerning the Siege at Oswestree (July 1644).
Wareham taken by the Parliament Forces. Also Collonel Mittons valiant Exploits certified by two several Letters dated at his Quarters (August 1644).
A True Relation of Two Great Victories obtained of the Enemy: The one by Sir William Brereton in Cheshire, The other by Sir John Meldrum in Lancashire (August 1644).
The Success of Our Cheshire Forces, as they came Related by Sir William Brereton's own pen (August 1644).
Letters From Sir William Brereton, Sir Thomas Middleton, Sir John Meldrum, Of the Great Victory (by God's providence), given them in raising the siege from before Montgomery-castle (September 1644).

(ii). Contemporary Newsbooks
A Diary, or an Exact Journal: 8-15 August 1644; 13 September 1644.
A Perfect Diurnall of some passages in Parliament: 25 March-1 April 1644; 12-19 August 1644; 9 September 1644.
Certaine Informations from Several Parts of the Kingdom: 19-26 June 1643.
Mercurius Aulicus (published in Oxford): 14 January 1643; 25 November 1643; 21 September 1644.
Mercurius Britanicus: 23-30 September 1644.
The Kingdomes Weekly Intelligencer: 24 September-1 October 1644.

The London Post: 3 September 1644; 24 September 1644.

The Perfect Occurrences of Parliament And Chief Collections of Letters: 16-23 August 1644; 6-13 September 1644; 3-10 October 1645.

The True Informer: 10-17 August 1644; 21-28 September 1644.

The Weekly Account: 18-24 September 1644.

(iii). Books and Edited Collections of Papers

Anon., *A List of Officers Claiming the Sixty Thousand Pounds, &c. Granted by his Majesty for the Relief of His Loyal and Indigent Party Truly* (1663).

Anon., *The Letters and Journals of Robert Baillie* (Edinburgh, 1841).

Anon., 'Various Documents relating to Montgomery Castle and Borough, in *Collections Historical and Archaeological Relating to Montgomeryshire and its Borders* (1881).

Anon., 'The Price Correspondence of Newtown Hall', in *Collections Historical and Archaeological relating to Montgomeryshire and its Borders* (1900).

Atkyns, R., *The Vindication of Richard Atkyns, Esquire* (1669).

Beaumont, W. (ed.), *A Discourse of the Warr in Lancashire* (Chetham Society, 1864).

Boyle, R., first Earl of Orrery, *A Treatise of the Art of War: Dedicated to the King's Most Excellent Majesty* (1677).

Carte, T. (ed.), *A Collection of Letters, Written by the Kings Charles I and II, The Duke of Ormonde, the Secretaries of State, the Marques of Clanricarde, and other Great Men, during the Troubles of Great Britain and Ireland* (1735).

Carte, T. (ed.), *A Collection of Original Letters and Papers, Concerning the Affairs of England, from the Year 1641 to 1660. Found among the Duke of Ormonde's Papers* (1739).

Carte, T., *The Life of James, Duke of Ormonde; Containing an account of the most remarkable affairs of his time, and particularly of Ireland under his government: with an appendix and collection of letters, serving to verify the most material facts in the said history. New Edition carefully compared with the original MSS* (Oxford, 1851).

Chadwick Healey, C.E.H. (ed.), *Bellum Civile: Hopton's Narratove of His Campaigns in the West (1642-1644)* (1902).

Day, W.A. (ed.), *The Pythouse Papers: Correspondence Concerning The Civil War, the Popish Plot and a Contested Election in 1680* (1879).

Dore, R.N. (ed.), *The Letter Books of Sir William Brereton, Volume I, January 31st–May 29th 1645* (Gloucester, 1984).

Firth, C.H. (ed.), 'The Journal of Prince Rupert's Marches, 5 September 1642 to 4 July 1646', *The English Historical Review* (1898).

Hamilton, W.D. (ed.) [*et al.*], *Calendar of State Papers, Domestic Series, of the Reign of Charles I, 1625-1649* (1858-97).

Historical Manuscripts Commission, *Fifth Report, Part I, Report and Appendix* (1876).

Historical Manuscripts Commission, *Thirteenth Report, Appendix Part I, The Manuscripts of his Grace the Duke of Portland, Volume I* (1891).

Historical Manuscripts Commission, *Twelfth Report, Appendix Part IX, Manuscripts of the Duke of Beaufort* (1891).

Historical Manuscripts Commission, *Fourteenth Report, Appendix Part VII, Manuscripts of the Marquis of Ormonde* (1895).

Journals of the House of Commons (1802).

Journals of the House of Lords (undated).

Mackay, W.D. (ed.), *The History of the Rebellion and Civil Wars in England begun in the Year 1641 by Edward Earl of Clarendon* (Oxford, 1888).

Malbon, T., 'Memorials of the Civil War in Cheshire and the Adjacent Counties by Thomas Malbon of Nantwich, Gent', (ed.) J. Hall, *The Record Society for the Publication of Original Documents relating to Lancashire and Cheshire* (1889).

Ogilby, J., *Britannia, or an Illustration of the Kingdom of England and Dominion of Wales by a Geographical and Historical Description of the Principal Roads thereof* (1675).

Rushworth, J., *Historical Collections of Private Passages of State* (1721).

Symonds, R., *Diary of The Marches of the Royal Army During the Great Civil War kept by Richard Symonds*, (ed.) C.E. Long (The Camden Society, 1859).

Walker, Sir Edward, *Historical Discourses upon Several Occasions* (1705).

Watts, W., *The Swedish Discipline: The Third Part* (1632).

Williams, R. (ed.), 'An Account of the Civil War in North Wales, Transcribed from the MS Notebook of William Maurice, esq., Preserved in the Wynnstay Library', *Archaeologica Cambrensis* (1846).

Secondary Sources

Anon., 'Place Names In and Around Montgomery', in *Collections Historical and Archaeological relating to Montgomeryshire and its Borders* (1891).

Abram, A., *The Battle of Montgomery 1644* (Bristol, 1993).

Archwilio: The Historic Environment Records of the Welsh Archaeological Trusts. Available (summer 2015): www.archwilio.org.uk.

Barratt, J., *Cavaliers, The Royalist Army at War, 1642-1646* (Stroud, 2000).

Barratt, J., *The Battle of York: Marston Moor 1644* (Stroud, 2002).

Barratt, J., *Cavalier Generals: King Charles and His Commanders in the English Civil War, 1642-46* (Barnsley, 2004).

Bennett, M., *The Civil Wars in Britain and Ireland: 1638-1651* (Oxford, 1996).

Burnham, H., *A Guide to Ancient and Historic Wales: Clwyd and Powys* (London, 1995).

Carlton, C., *This Seat of Mars: War and The British Isles, 1485-1746* (New Haven and London, 2011).

Clwyd-Powys Archaeological Trust (CPAT), *Historic Landscape Characterisation: The Vale of Montgomery.* Available (summer 2015): www.cpat.org.uk/projects.

Cust, R., *Charles I And The Aristocracy, 1625-1642* (Cambridge, 2013).

Dictionary of Welsh Biography. Available (summer 2015): wbo.yba.llgc.org.uk.

Dore, R.N., 'Sir Thomas Myddelton's Attempted Conquest of Powys, 1644-45', *The Montgomeryshire Collections, Transactions of the Powys-Land Club* (1961-2).

Evans, D., *Montgomery 1644: The Story of the Castle and Civil War Battle* (Llanidloes, undated).

Fletcher, A., *Reform in the Provinces, The Government of Stuart England* (New Haven and London, 1986).

Foard, G., *Naseby The Decisive Campaign* (2nd edition, Barnsley, 2004).

Foard, G., and R. Morris, *The Archaeology of English Battlefields: Conflict in the Pre-Industrial Landscape* (York, 2012).

Gentles, I., *The English Revolution and the Wars in the Three Kingdoms 1638-1652* (Harlow, 2007).

Gaunt, P., *A Nation Under Siege; The Civil War in Wales 1642-48* (London, 1991).

Gaunt, P., "One of the Goodliest and Strongest Places that I ever looked upon": Montgomery in the Civil War', in (ed.) D. Dunn, *War and Society in Medieval and Early Modern Britain* (Liverpool, 2000).

Gratton, J.M., *The Parliamentarian and Royalist War Effort in Lancashire 1642-1651* (Manchester, 2010).

Hackett, M., *Lost Battlefields of Britain* (Stroud, 2005).

Hackett, M., *Lost Battlefields of Wales* (Stroud, 2014).

Hibbert, C., *Cavaliers & Roundheads: The English at War, 1642-1649* (London, 1993).

Hopper, A.J., 'Black Tom': Sir Thomas Fairfax and The English Revolution* (Manchester, 2007).

Howell, A., 'The Roads, Bridges, Canals and Railways of Montgomeryshire', *Collections Historical and Archaeological relating to Montgomeryshire and its Borders* (1875).

Hutton, R., *The Royalist War Effort 1642-1646* (2nd edition, London, 2003).

Keegan, J., *The Face of Battle: A Study of Agincourt, Waterloo and The Somme* (Harmondsworth, 1976).

Markham, C.R., *Life of Robert Fairfax of Steeton, 1666-1725* (London, 1885).

Matthews, H.C.G. and B. Harrison (eds.), *Oxford Dictionary of National Biography* (40 Volumes, Oxford, 2004).

Morrill, J., 'Sir William Brereton and England's Wars of Religion', *The Journal of British Studies* (1985).

Newman, P.R., *The Old Service: Royalist Regimental Colonels and the Civil War, 1642-46* (Manchester, 1993).

Parry, E., *Royal Visits and Progresses to Wales and the Border Counties of Cheshire, Salop, Hereford and Monmouth* (London, 1851).

Peachey, S., *The Mechanics of Infantry Combat in the First English Civil War* (Bristol, 1992).

Phillips, J.R., *Memorials of The Civil War in Wales and the Marches, 1642-1649* (2 Volumes, London, 1874).

Roberts, K., *Pike and Shot Tactics, 1590-1660* (Oxford, 2010).

Silvester, R.J., C.H.R. Martin and S. Watson, *Historic Settlements In Montgomeryshire,* CPAT Report No. 1134 (Welshpool, 2012).

Stoyle, M., *Soldiers And Strangers: An Ethnic History of the English Civil War* (New Haven and London, 2005).

Tincey, J., *Marston Moor 1644: The beginning of the End* (London, 2003).

Tucker, N., *North Wales and Chester in the Civil War* (Ashbourne, 2003).

Walters, M.J., and K. Hunnisett, *The Civil War Battlefield at Montgomery, Powys, Archaeological Assessment*, CPAT Report No. 142 (Welshpool, 1995).

Warburton, E., *Memoirs of Prince Rupert and the Cavaliers* (London, 1849).

Young, P., *Marston Moor 1644 – The Campaign and the Battle* (Moreton-in Marsh, 1997).